Field Gu *Happiness for Women*

Barbara Ann Kipfer

Guilford, Connecticut
An imprint of The Globe Pequot Press

GPP Life gives women answers they can trust.

Copyright © 2009 by Barbara Ann Kipfer

GPP Life is an imprint of The Globe Pequot Press.

Cover design by Georgiana Goodwin
Text designed by Libby Kingsbury

Library of Congress Cataloging-in-Publication Data is available on file.

ISBN 978-1-59921-488-7

Printed in the United States of America

10 9 8 7 6 5 4 3 2 1

Introduction

Field Guide to Happiness for Women is a book about using interesting tools to discover what makes you happy and sets you on a course to "choose" happiness. Being a woman is often challenging—we are pulled in many directions at the same time. Raising children, pursuing careers, caring for aging parents, and saving for retirement; these are just a few of the challenges we face. But, even with all these hurdles to overcome, choosing to be happy is still a choice we can make. Every aspect of life is touched upon in the 205 mini chapters within this book. Topics such as food and exercise, ways of thinking, simplifying, and taking action; meditation and spiritual pursuits; gratitude and kindness—205 ways to appreciate life, in all its messy, imperfect excellence.

Each one of the 205 mini chapters in *Field Guide to Happiness for Women* encourages readers to contemplate their everyday choices and tells them how to gear them toward happiness. Whether you read this book from front to back, discuss it with friends, or just pick it up and look at a chapter, you will see its usefulness in making happiness your personal choice. The book is intended to inspire each reader to create a personal path that is joyful. The emotions and circumstances facing all women make such a field guide a welcome tool. Sometimes we need a little help or a reminder of how to achieve happiness. While there are plenty of books about fitness and style for women, few are targeted to motivate, inspire, and comfort them. Enjoy!

1. Eat Quality Food

No matter how you feel about your body and your weight, you will be happier if you eat quality (fresh, healthful, nutritious) food. This has been described in detail in books like *French Women Don't Get Fat,* so you're probably already familiar with the idea. You should be eating attractive, good-tasting, fresh, quality food at restaurants and at home.

Eating out at restaurants is an important social activity today. When you lead a busy life, eating out can be a relaxing and satisfying experience. Instead of going to eat at a chain restaurant, for a few more dollars you could go to a quality restaurant and have quality food. Isn't that a more satisfying way to spend your money on food? Why spend it on a forgettable meal at a so-so restaurant?

The same is true for what you eat at home. If you make meals from fresh ingredients, you know it will taste better and be more satisfying to all who eat it. It will be a higher-quality experience at the table, and even in your body—whose tissues benefit from the nutrients in better-quality food. In today's world, it only takes a little effort to find quality foods at a store near you. There is a major trend for stores to stock locally grown and organic foods no matter what part of the country you live in. In most cases, buying quality food is all about breaking a bad habit and replacing it with a good one. Once you begin to purchase fresh ingredients, you will feel a difference within yourself.

It's important to also be aware of the miracle of food and how it finds its way to your table. And then there's the miracle of the body—the fact that you have a digestive, nutrient-absorbing, and elimination system that processes your food each day. Eat slowly and mindfully, ever aware of the pleasure that comes from your food.

2. Walk More

Walk more for better health and happiness. Walking has been around since we became upright mammals. We are made to walk. There are many benefits to walking, both physical and mental. Physically, walking helps make your metabolism more efficient, thus helping you manage your weight. Walking can also decrease your risk of a heart attack and help control your blood pressure. Walking strengthens the heart and lets it work more efficiently. Studies have also shown that walking can help lower your risk of a stroke, boost good cholesterol, reduce your risk of breast cancer and diabetes, lower your stress level, improve sleep, relieve some types of arthritis, and protect against hip fractures, to name a few. Walking is an independent activity, free from equipment, trainer, or coach, and, in most cases, free of charge. And most people who exercise by walking are doing it outside, enjoying nature, breathing fresh air, and appreciating the scenery.

The mental benefits of walking are just as important as the physical ones. Walking helps you get to know yourself better. If you choose to think while you walk, you may come up with solutions to problems or discover insights into your being. You can also make walking a type of meditation. This can be done by observing nature with all of your senses, or by paying attention to your every step or every breath. The art of walking meditation is to learn to be aware as you walk, to use the natural movement of walking to cultivate mindfulness and be in the present moment. Whether you are a walking thinker or meditator, you will be able to see the benefits you receive from walking quite clearly. Even if you are a fast-paced walker, walking still contributes to taking an overall slower approach to life.

Getting into the habit of walking more is certainly easier in better weather and safer places, but you can be creative in adding more walking time—even if it is walking in circles in your basement. Many people add walking to their lunch hour or make it social by walking with a friend or partner. A great, safe place to walk is on a public school track when no sports programs are taking place. Your tax dollars help to pay for the track, so take advantage of this great resource to walk more. Whatever way you choose to walk more, walk in peace.

3. Lighten Up

This may sound flippant, but if you think about yourself being just one person in the six billion currently on Earth, and then place yourself within the context of all human beings dating back millions of years, you realize your "importance" is really rather small. You are put here on Earth to find your passions and strengths, to find a way to contribute to the world, and to be happy for your own sake and for those around you. Reminding yourself to lighten up is helpful, especially when you take things too seriously, when you get angry about petty matters, or when you spend too much time thinking and worrying about yourself.

Instead of being serious or angry or otherwise upset, try to find either some humor in the situation, or at least a lesson. If your opinion differs from someone else's, it's probably not imperative that the other person understand your point of view. Explaining it over and over will not clarify your position. It is really true that the only person you can change, in any way, is yourself.

Think about this: Most things are not worth getting upset about. If you take a circumstance that is upsetting and ask yourself if it will matter (or if you'll even remember it) in a day, a week, a month, a year, or ten years—well, you know that the majority of the time, the answer will be "No, it won't matter." Yesterday you worried about wearing the right outfit today. But tomorrow when someone asks you what you wore the day before, you most likely won't remember what the outfit was! We often get into a tizzy about things that don't matter in the grand scheme of things, when we would most benefit from letting it go and lightening up.

Examine your opinions and harsh feelings; watch them form and then melt like snowflakes. Let go of those rigid opinions and bad feelings. You will actually feel lighter. Your example of "lightening up" will not go unnoticed by family, friends, and coworkers. You will not only help yourself, but you will also have a tremendously positive impact on all those around you.

4. Create a Support System

Things can always go wrong, and situations can get confusing; It's Murphy's Law. It is a really good idea to have a support system in place, a person or persons from whom you can seek counsel. This can consist of your family or friends, but can also include groups, like a church organization, fellow gym members, or even an online community. It is often true that when you perceive something to be a problem, as soon as you describe it or talk about it with someone else, your burden seems lighter.

You have to be smart about who you choose to turn to, depending on the type of support you are seeking. If you have a problem involving a child, you would not expect someone who does not have children to understand that problem. So don't frustrate yourself by expecting people who don't share your frame of reference to understand. You need allies who are going through or have gone through similar situations.

Look for people who are kind, honest, and generous. Maybe they have accomplished something you would also like to accomplish, like losing weight. Maybe they are working with the same types of problems and frustrations, like fellow moms. It's important to select your support system wisely. Even if you only have one support person, it's still better than none. And be sure to appreciate the numerous people who gave you guidance and support today. Just as you may need a support system, remember that other people may need one, too. Be aware when someone makes you part of their support system. Treat them with the kindness, honesty, and generosity that you would expect to receive. It is a two-way street. Instead of misery loves company, try *happiness loves company*.

5. Include Six Tastes in Every Meal

There is an ancient healing system called Ayurveda, which deals a lot with eating, knowing your body and personality type, and then selecting foods that balance your body and give you the energy you need. The tastes of different foods have a physiological effect on us. Ayurveda says that one reason people overeat is that most of us do not get all six tastes in our main meals (lunch and dinner). The six tastes are *sweet* (qualities are oily, cooling, and heavy), *salty* (qualities are oily, heating, and heavy), *bitter* (qualities are dry and light), *sour* (qualities are oily, heating, liquid, and light), *pungent* (qualities are drying, light, and heating), and *astringent* (qualities are cooling, drying, and heavy). You can see how our diets favor the sweet and salty tastes and often exclude the others.

For the body to be satisfied and balanced, it requires not only sweet and salty flavors, but also bitter (citrus rind, leafy greens, spices like turmeric), pungent (cayenne, garlic, ginger, onions), astringent (apples, beans, cabbage, potatoes), and sour (lemons, pickles, plums, tomatoes, yogurt) tastes.

Including all six tastes in every lunch and dinner causes you to eat a variety of foods and therefore obtain optimal nutrition. It's part of our nature, within our body, to want these six tastes. Since most of us have concentrated on sweet and salty, it will require some work and habit-breaking willpower to achieve this. But it can be done, and learning a bit about Ayurveda helps. There are little tricks to aid you, like having chutney (an Indian condiment) around. This condiment adds the missing tastes to any meal.

6. Stop Comparing

Comparing is just too darned easy; there are billions of people to compare yourself to, and the media bombard us every day with all types—rich, famous, beautiful, accomplished. Comparing is an exercise in futility. And it separates us from others when, in truth, we are all interconnected.

You are you. You miss out when you compare yourself to other people, when you wish for things to be different. If you spend time comparing yourself to others, you are taking away the one thing you really need, which is unconditional love for yourself. In every situation where you feel discomfort, it is because you want something to be different. You are grasping after an idea you have about the way your life should be, rather than simply being present for what *is*.

If watching TV and reading magazines make you feel upset because you see people who look the way you want to look, or have the kind of life you desire, then maybe you should do or read something different. Without the comparisons, your life will be much better.

You can love yourself right now, just the way you are. There is no need to compare yourself with others. Others have a right to be rich, famous, beautiful, or accomplished—but so do you, and those labels come from your own mind. You can believe in yourself and love yourself for all you are, right now in this moment.

7. Discover Yoga

Yoga addresses the whole person, improving the state of both body and mind. If you have not discovered yoga yet, please give it a try. If you picture it as something designed for those who are not overweight and who are flexible, you are wrong. Almost all of the thousand yoga poses can be done by the average human being.

Yoga increases your endurance, strength, and flexibility. The postures benefit breathing, muscles, joints, connective tissue, organs, and glands—so that every body function improves in efficiency. And because the mind is involved in yoga practice, along with the physical benefits, you also become mentally more calm and flexible. You may even find that practicing yoga will help you make gradual changes to a healthier, more balanced diet without even realizing that this is happening. The first step to discovering yoga involves taking an honest look at yourself. Look at how you like to exercise: alone or with others, for a long or short time, early in the day or later. There are many different types of yoga and many ways in which to practice it. Next, determine if you will feel comfortable practicing yoga in a yoga studio, or if you'd feel more comfortable practicing it at home. If you think you'd like to practice yoga in a studio, whether you live in a large or small city or town, you will be able to find a yoga studio that offers classes close by. Try a few to make sure you are comfortable with the setting and the teacher. If you think you'd prefer practicing yoga at home, there are many excellent books to use and DVDs to rent or purchase that will get you on your way. By understanding how you exercise best and what your comfort level is, you will increase the odds of sticking to a yoga program because you'll enjoy it. You will be able to see and feel the benefits.

Whether you practice in a studio or at home, you will certainly feel happier and healthier by adding yoga to your life. You will feel more limber, energized, and relaxed. The breathing, relaxation, and meditation exercises will contribute greatly to your overall well-being.

8. Do Things Now

Procrastination is not a pretty word. You probably don't like hearing it. Tending to the little things in life before they become big things doesn't take more of your time—it actually takes less. Even true procrastinators can admit they don't procrastinate to save time. And, if pressed, they would also admit that putting things off doesn't make the tasks any easier.

If you get used to taking care of things *now*, you will be taking responsibility for your life. You cannot count on tomorrow. Today, this moment, is all you can count on. And tomorrow is less likely to be a great day if you carry over a bunch of stuff that you should have dealt with the day before. The only truly good reasons to wait before tending to something is if you need more information; if you are upset or angry and need to calm down in order to deal with a situation; or, if something is really not your business anyway.

When most people think of doing things now, they think of chores or responsibilities. Rushing to "get things done" can add stress to your daily life, which is not going to lead to more happiness. But there is another aspect of doing things now that will reduce stress and add to happiness: If you think you owe someone an apology, an explanation, or even your two cents' worth, you probably do. Dealing with mistakes and mix-ups right away is the best policy, just like honesty. Apologizing to someone you offended produces marvelous and immediate relief for both of you. It is best to apologize immediately, as soon as you recognize your thoughtlessness and lack of mindfulness. Life works better when you make restitution and amends, even if others do not do the same. You know that sometimes even your best intentions will not keep you from screwing up. At least by addressing the issue right away, you know you have done what you can to rectify things. It makes you the bigger human being. By doing things now, you will create a more efficient life for yourself and greatly reduce your stress level. You will not only be amazed by how much better you feel, but also by how much more you can accomplish.

9. Simplify

Simplifying is talked about a lot, but it is not the easiest thing to do! Yes, staying busy is good in many ways. You engage in the world and with other people. You are likely using your mind in a good way. However, for some, being constantly occupied becomes an obsession: If you are busy, you must be important. If you are busy, you must be accomplishing something useful. While those things could be true, can you see that simplifying and taking on fewer obligations might give you more time to focus on what truly makes you happy?

On the other hand, a lot of people complain that they are too busy. There is a fine line here, and it is important to be aware of it and to remind yourself that it is a good thing to simplify your life.

Being overwhelmed causes many other problems, like overeating or mindless eating, not concentrating on tasks, not listening well to others, not being fully in any moment, even when you are exercising, brushing your teeth, or driving.

Possessions can complicate your life, too. Acquiring things costs time and money, and takes your attention away from people and projects that truly mean something to you. Do you buy things to keep up with the Joneses? To "define" who you are? Do you buy things to get others to love you—to fill an emotional hole in your being? Remember: Something only feels new for a little while, and then it becomes "that old thing." It is very easy to get caught up in the endless hamster wheel of buying things and then having to pay for them.

Simplifying and letting go of excess is about gradually changing your habits. It means cleaning out emotional as well as physical clutter. Over time, letting go and simplifying will just feel right to you. Our lives are often filled with a million things to do—and to consume—and these things distract us from simple living. When you pay attention and become mindful, you marvel at the simple things in life that you once passed over. Consuming less and living simply are the true conditions for happiness.

10. Play

We often feel funny as adults when we allow "play" into our lives. But, when you think about it, you spent around twenty years perfecting your ability to play, so why ignore it or shuffle it aside after that? We are meant to play our whole lives, as written about most poignantly by Diane Ackerman in *Deep Play*.

Have some fun. Be silly. Laugh. You can find funny movies, jokes, comic strips, sporting activities or hobbies, or whatever works best for you to get some humor and play into your life. Laughing fills your body with all kinds of great chemicals that make you feel content and complete. Can you remember how good it feels to experience a laugh attack?

Don't overlook opportunities to play. Watch how little children play, and learn from them. Do puzzles if you like them, or draw in a sketchbook. Annotate your books with comments and opinions. Change your exercise to be more playful. You can become more playful by simply doing what you like to do and not apologizing for it. Even spending fifteen minutes reading a gossipy magazine can be an indulgence that gives you pleasure. Play is personal.

Play is needed to balance life, whether you are a child (whose "work" is school) or an adult. Play makes you appreciate work, and vice versa. Of course, the best of all possible worlds is when you feel that the universe is your playground. To love what you do and feel that it matters—how could anything be more fun?

11. Be Kind to Yourself

We all get down on ourselves—and sometimes, others do it for us. That's when you have to dig deep and be kind to yourself. Remind yourself that your feelings, or those of others, are temporary. You need patience, because you could have a string of bad days, not just one.

Treat yourself the way you would treat a child you love very much. With the child, you would be patient and kind. You would be helpful. You might indulge the child, but you would know when to say no. You can do the very same for yourself to get through tough times without self-inflicted pain and suffering.

Maybe some spiritual reading will speak to you right now, even if it is just uplifting quotations or some poetry. There's also plenty in philosophy, psychology, and spirituality writings that may address what you are going through. Remember to be kind and supportive to yourself. When you realize the transient nature of these feelings or difficulties, you will be able to find joy even in the midst of a troubled time. *This too shall pass* is a cliché for a reason.

You have to generate love and compassion for yourself first. The nourishment that comes from being kind to yourself is the kind of food that stays with you.

12. Conserve Your Energy

We all could do with a bit more energy, right? It would be unusual these days to meet someone who did not feel tired or exhausted several times a week, both mentally and physically. We take on a lot of responsibility in our lives (sometimes too much). Quite often, we take our lives too seriously. And we shoulder burdens and problems and either don't ask for help, or don't know where or how to ask for it. Sometimes we take care of ourselves, but other times we eat food that does not increase our energy, or we don't exercise and find ourselves lagging. If we don't remember to rest our minds occasionally, that can also deplete our energy resources.

One thing you can do is become more realistic as to your personal responsibilities and the seriousness of the situations you face. Another is to let go of problems you can do nothing about. This is not as hard as you think. You just need to stop and remind yourself to do these things, and you will start to cultivate more energy. Eating healthy, fresh, quality food helps. Exercising daily also helps. Adding time for meditation is just as important for your mind as exercise is for your body. Doing other things, like taking a hot bath or shower and getting a good night's sleep, can help, too.

There are a few other things you can do, mainly having to do with speech. We talk too much. We drain ourselves talking about minutiae, gossiping, and preaching to others. Give your mouth a rest and you'll have more energy. The other energy drainer is expectations. When you expect too much from yourself and others—actually, when you expect *anything*—you will likely be disappointed. You can't control others, and you really don't have control over your own life, either. Everything and everyone are interconnected, so whatever you "expect" can suddenly be changed by something or someone else.

Fatigue can result from a day filled with wasted thought, anxiety and worry, anger and resentment. All of these negative feelings can sap your energy. When you let go of these unmindful thoughts and actions, your feelings of tiredness will dissipate.

13. Face the Unresolved

Most of the time, we exist with unresolved problems. The question is, how do we handle it? Do the problems gnaw at us, thereby causing us to snap at people over a totally unrelated matter? Do they cause us to wake up in the middle of the night or lose our concentration when at work? The ability to coexist with the unresolved has great practical value. Has there ever been a single day in your life when everything was "perfect"? Doubtful.

Most unresolved problems are irritations. Even solvable problems seldom have instant answers. Maybe your husband got mad over something you did and is not speaking to you, even though you apologized. Maybe you made an error on something at work and you discover it over the weekend—meaning you can't resolve it until Monday. Sometimes the unresolved can be more serious: being in limbo over a medical test result, or being unsure of the health or safety of someone we love. We can build courage to deal with the more substantial problems by learning to coexist with unresolved trivial matters.

It's always something. There will always be something to work on, something that could be better. But you are not "in denial" if you see a problem and behave normally in spite of it. It is better to fence off a problem so that it does not seep into other areas of your life. A job problem should not accompany you to the family dinner table.

You might want to talk with someone you trust about an unresolved situation. Or you can write in your journal or blog about it. Then, take whatever actions you can to address the issue before you make a decision to let it go. Turn away and do something else, something happy or something else that needs to be attended to. The idea is to seek to be grounded in calmness and moment-to-moment awareness. With this awareness, you will likely feel more creative and able to see new options, discover alternative solutions to problems, and be better able to maintain your balance and perspective in trying circumstances.

14. Add Adventure

You may scoff at the admonishment to add more adventure to your life, but adventure need not be reserved for the young. We are a sheltered culture, and often cocoon ourselves in our living rooms and bedrooms with electronic gadgets and central heating and air-conditioning. We feel safe with the protection we build up around our lives, keeping many risks at bay.

Yet we ache for adventure. When we were young, driving hours to do something fun was no problem. Trying a new restaurant was not a major decision. Going on a vacation without a phone or computer was normal. Finding a parking space at an event was not even a thought, let alone a roadblock to doing something. We made our lives more interesting by trying new things, and then we let that part of life go when we started to focus on our career and children.

But why? We're always happier at work if our leisure time is fun. Our children are always happier if we are happier adults.

Think about what you would add to your life in the way of adventure if you could, and then start to take steps to add these elements. You could start small, by finding more adventurous ways of doing things that you already do: try an ethnic restaurant for lunch instead of the hamburger stand; go to an evening movie to get out of the habit of just going to bargain matinees; drive instead of fly someplace for a vacation; do anything else to take yourself off the beaten path. Don't be afraid to be adventurous!

Your life can become more exuberant by adding stimulating people, places, and events to your daily routine.

15. Enlarge Your World

Part of what I wanted to show in my book *14,000 Things to be Happy About* is that you don't have to have everything, see everything, go everywhere, etc., to be happy. Even without oodles of money or the adventurous spirit of great explorers, you can still enlarge your world.

Though travel is the more direct way to gain a global perspective, there is no reason why you cannot do the same by reading, learning, watching documentaries and movies, and talking to people. Not everyone who travels enjoys the experience; even though they may be in direct contact with a culture, they may not come away with a real sense of it. Not too long ago, I watched a movie called *The Namesake*. There was a powerful scene in which a young man described how his grandfather taught him that books are a way to travel without moving an inch.

You can tour the world by reading newspapers and Web site content created in other places, and by going to museums to see the art and artifacts of other countries. You can study a foreign language, shop in ethnic and exotic markets, and read many books that will explain the beliefs, attitudes, folkways, traditions, and customs of other cultures. And certainly you can talk to others who are immigrants or whose families continue to maintain their culture while living in America.

Just like scientists study other worlds through telescopes and microscopes, you can learn to expand your world by using tools other than travel. The whole world is your teacher.

16. Find a Sacred Spot

Find a way to create a sacred spot for yourself. Ideally, it is a room, but very few of us can afford to set aside that much space. Alternatively, a corner of a room or a special chair is just as good. Selecting a sacred spot for inner exploration is something you do to nourish your spiritual life.

This sacred spot encourages a spiritual practice that might otherwise be overlooked because of your busy life. Cultivating your spiritual side has benefits that spill over into all areas of your life. You will intuitively choose a spot that will make sense in relation to your home life and others who live there.

In this spot, you can have a place to sit, a cushion or pillow, an altar or table (or even a window ledge), flowers, a candle, a statue, or other meaningful items. Or it can be Zen-like and open. You can go there in the morning, especially if you awaken before others. You can go there at night, designating a time that you take for yourself. Ask others to be considerate of this time in your sacred spot. If it is chilly there, add a blanket or robe you can put on.

Joseph Campbell said this:

> You must have a room or a certain hour of the day or so where you do not know what was in the morning paper . . . a place where you can simply experience and bring forth what you are, and what you might be. . . . At first you may find nothing's happening. . . . But if you have a sacred place and use it, take advantage of it, something will happen.

17. Find Things To Be Nostalgic About

There is a part of each of us that needs to interact with things in the past. Though we aim to center ourselves in the present moment, we can also choose to take a moment to remember the past. Much comfort can be found in history, in things and activities that made us happy. There's so much change in the world, and we can appreciate that. But we can also appreciate past happiness.

One way is to keep a list of things to be nostalgic about:

Jerry West, basketball player
old tintypes
Mickey Mouse's gloved hands
sleeping caps
making your own candles

videocassette recorders

"California Dreamin'," a song by the Mamas and the Papas

getting your Christmas Club check

the Ides of March

velvet-curtained theaters

a toddler's first jumbo pencil

the Senate Watergate hearings

aperitif posters of the 1920s

the movie *My Big Fat Greek Wedding*

an un-busy mall

the pleasurable pull of the past

an old pool parlor

Twinkles the elephant

the first cookbook, published in 1475

Miss Piggy's pretentious attitude

the flaking paint on a rustic old bench

a phone with a long cord or a cordless phone

shoe shines at the airport

sea monkeys, Chia Pets, and Pet Rocks

You get the idea.

Another way to appreciate nostalgia is to have some timeless objects around the house—maybe antiques, an afghan your grandmother made, a Princess telephone in the basement. Each has a story to tell and can be a conversation piece when you have visitors. You can even revive some of the "lost arts" as hobbies: baking bread from scratch, playing checkers, knitting, or doing a paint-by-number painting.

18. Practice Right Speech

Right Speech is one of the elements in Buddha's Eightfold Path to Enlightenment. The concept of Right Speech is to refrain from lying, divisive speech, harsh speech, and senseless speech. Practicing Right Speech is a very valuable tool in achieving happiness.

Because the effects of speech are not as immediately evident as those of bodily action, its importance and potential are sometimes overlooked. A little reflection will show that speech and the written word can have enormous consequences for good or for harm. Speech can ruin lives, create enemies, and start wars, or it can give wisdom, heal divisions, and create peace. We can appreciate the need to make our speech more "right."

We too often express pessimism or criticism that does not need to be voiced. We make comments about what other people say, really, just to hear ourselves talk. We don't stop to ask whether we really need to say what we say, or ask ourselves whether what we are about to say is kind or useful. We blurt out opinions that are hurtful, even if they are "honest." And we lie, talk about others when they are not there, exaggerate, put down and diminish people and things, and talk in unnecessary absolutes and superlatives. Feeling the sting of recognition yet?

Well, it is true for each and every one of us that there is room for improvement in this area. Right Speech can greatly improve your life and the lives of those around you. Well-spoken words are

- *spoken at the proper time*
- *spoken in line with the truth*
- *spoken gently*

- *spoken beneficially*
- *spoken with a friendly heart*

Use these five characteristics as reminders on the path toward Right Speech. And also remember that much of the time, silence really is golden.

19. *Ask for What You Want or Need*

You just gotta ask for what you want or need, unless you can supply it yourself—or unless you let go of wanting, which takes practice and time. But, otherwise, you have to ask. Human beings are interconnected and interdependent, and it's pretty much impossible to have a happy life if you don't ask other people for help. When you ask for what you want, the answer may be no. If you don't ask, the answer is always no.

No one can read your mind. Hints and insinuations don't work, either. It is not a sign of weakness to assert yourself and ask for what you want or need. Yes, you have to be prepared for rejection, or for someone to insensitively ignore your request. But, with practice— especially with loved ones who may not be used to your honest requests for what you want—you will soon start getting positive responses. Ask politely and directly for what you want. No raising your voice or whining.

Since asking for what you want or need frequently involves loved ones, it is important to note that asking for what you want or need may reduce many family arguments. When you ask, you eliminate the need for someone to read your mind. If this process is not abused and the request is reasonable, most loved ones will be eager to give you what you want and need. In fact, they will experience a sense of happiness because they are able to make you happy or satisfied. As this becomes a habit, with all parties asking for what they want or need, the relationships should improve and the love grow.

In return, you also need to respond positively to other people's requests as often as you can. You contribute positively to the world every time you clearly ask for what you want or need. By this, we are not talking about making someone your servant. If you need to talk, you ask for a time to talk. If you need to get out of the house and have a date with your partner, then simply ask. Even if you need a day alone, however selfish it may seem, it is something you should ask for. These things may rejuvenate you and make you feel more appreciative of your life, and, ultimately, make you happier.

20. Slow Down

The journey is more important than the arrival, and, especially, enjoying the journey. The only way to really accomplish this is to slow down. The only thing we are ever hurrying toward is the arrival, the destination, the end result. To cultivate the habit of slowing down, becoming unhurried, means that you also have to have your priorities straight. You know that your time with people, projects, even yourself is important.

Whenever I think about the fact that the journey is more important than the arrival, I remember going out to dinner with my husband many years ago. It was a beautiful late afternoon in the fall. The kids were with their grandparents. The restaurant was about thirty minutes from our house. My husband was driving, and I was reading a book and looking out the window at the foliage. Not too many words were spoken on the drive, but the feeling of happiness was overwhelming. I was truly enjoying the journey. After all these years, I can't remember the meal I had (the destination), but I feel joy when remembering the journey.

In a world of speed, it may be hard to admit this would benefit you. It's exhilarating to be busy, to accomplish a lot. But in doing that, are you losing touch with what you value most? Think about how your life would be with more peace, freedom, relaxation, and even a little emptiness.

Can you eliminate some of the things you do, like reading Internet news sites more than once a day? Can you leave for work a little earlier so it won't be as stressful? Can you plan a few midweek meals so that the ingredients are on hand? How about slowing down when you wash the dishes or brush your teeth? You can experience everyday routines in a more pleasant way, and you can also open up some space in your day for more pleasurable activities. You might even find out that slowing down means your memory works better—that you save time because you remember to take things with you that you'll need, and to write things down that you'll need to know. You will likely feel more energy and creativity pouring into your life, just from slowing down and enjoying the journey.

21. Be Specific

Life really is about the little things. Instructions are needed and used for so many everyday activities: how to type, how to use a computer, how to make a cup of coffee, how to brush your teeth, even how to read for comprehension. Knowing this, you have to admit that the specifics—the details—are helpful and necessary to completing activities. Now take this process one step further and practice being specific about what you really want and need. If it works for completing activities, it may work at helping you achieve more happiness, too.

Being specific about what you really want and need is important, just like buying the right ingredients for the dish you plan to make for dinner, or ordering the right size sheets for the bed. It takes courage to be specific about what you want in your life, what you need to be happy. It also has an element of common sense. Why be surprised about outcomes if you don't need to be?

If you want to be unhappy, you let your teenager go out and say, "Be home early." Or you say to the hairdresser, "Cut a little off." If you want to be happy, you say what time the teenager is supposed to be home, and exactly how much for the hairdresser to trim. Maybe there are certain things that don't matter to you, but in most cases, you *do* know what you want and you need to take responsibility for saying what it is. By being specific, you also take pressure off the people you are interacting with. They cannot read your mind, and it is unfair for you to assume that they can. When they know exactly what you mean, then they can behave or perform a task in an appropriate manner.

Being precise in all your intentions, speech, and actions takes practice. In both large and small matters, if you are true to your deepest principles, your integrity will be a gift to others.

22. Appreciate Details

The details of life are what the book 14,000 Things to be Happy About and the Web site www.thingstobehappyabout.com are all about. If you don't appreciate the details, then you miss the joy of the tiny things. If you just want *more* and *bigger*, you will be discontented. When you look at the book or the Web site and see a random list of things to be happy about, certain ones will jump out at you as personal and distinctive. It's important to know that those details make you happy. You also need to stay open to new ones.

You set goals based on the big picture, but the real joy comes from the details. The best way to appreciate and relish the details in life is to write a list, journal, diary, or blog. Writing things down is always better than relying on memory, however long it gets. You can share it with others now, or leave it for your kids and grandkids to read someday. You will be able to return to your list from time to time and relive the joy of your entries. You will remember the details surrounding your thoughts and experiences. It is your own personal time capsule!

Mindfulness means loving all the details of your life. Keeping a list of things to be happy about becomes a habit that makes you find joy in the little things.

23. Seek Out Positive Influences

If you want to be a positive person, seek out people and activities with those same qualities. Remember, like particles attract. Surrounding yourself with this kind of optimistic energy will help you achieve a more positive life. If you want happiness, take your future into your own hands. Actively seek positive influences that will help you achieve your fullest potential. Don't just sit in the giant barber chair, letting a stranger spin you around and have free rein at reshaping your head. Choose your barber (and your company) carefully, and face that mirror! You are the one who has to live with it.

This includes surrounding yourself with positive friends and fostering relationships with people at work who have an optimistic attitude and a constructive impact on your life. Positive thinking is contagious. Researchers continue to explore the effects of positive thinking and optimism on health. It's still unclear why people who engage in positive thinking experience these health benefits, but one theory maintains that having a positive outlook enables you to cope better with stressful situations, which then reduces the harmful effects of stress on your body.

Periodically during the day, stop and evaluate what you are thinking. If you find that your thoughts are mainly negative, try to find a way to put a positive spin on them.

Start by following one simple rule: Don't say anything to yourself that you wouldn't say to anyone else. Follow that with another simple rule: If you don't have something nice to say, don't say anything at all. Both of these rules are easy to follow, and with a little practice will become second nature.

A good habit to get used to that will improve your outlook is to practice positive self-talk. This involves using milder wording, changing negative or neutral statements to positive, and changing self-limiting statements to questions. Say "I'm doing fine." When your state of mind is generally optimistic, you're better able to handle everyday stress in a constructive way. That ability may contribute to the widely observed health benefits of positive thinking.

24. Perform Happy Activities

Fill your life with positive activities on a very regular basis. Talk to, or better yet, get together with a positive friend. Go to or rent a funny movie. Though the act of getting out is often therapeutic, you can enjoy a pay-per-view Marx Brothers movie almost any night of the week.

Play happy music, like Broadway show tunes. Do some free writing or writing in a journal about happy stuff. You can add on many other suggestions to this, as what you consider happy activities is very personal. You can look at the random lists at www .thingstobehappyabout.com, and suddenly you will see something that you would like to do, read, listen to.

Interestingly, many of the things that bring happiness are also things that relieve stress, such as exercise, expressing creativity, maintaining supportive friendships, keeping an organized home, and enjoying your work. Incorporating activities known to increase over-all happiness can give you short-term stress relief, and the lasting gains of a happy life. And when you incorporate into your life a general state of happiness, and make a habit of the lifestyle features that promote it, you'll be better able to weather future stress in your life.

Look at these areas for happy activities for yourself: health, goals and values, spiritual life, money, work, play, learning, creativity, helping others, love, friendship, children and family, home, neighborhood. Can you list three to five happy activities in each?

25. Keep a Journal

Henry David Thoreau was one of America's greatest thinkers and philosophers, and one of his biggest influences (and his great friend) was Ralph Waldo Emerson. Upon meeting Thoreau, Emerson suggested that he begin to keep a journal. Thoreau did so, on an almost-daily basis. Luckily for us Thoreau took Emerson's advice. My advice to you is the same. This is my way of inspiring you to begin that journal that will help you lead a happier life.

One of the most direct means for dealing with the mind is to write in a journal, on both your good days and bad days. It's a diary, yes, but it's even more useful as a place to clear out the clutter of your mind.

On bad days, you can enter your concerns, commentary, and criticisms, and then choose to leave them there; often, you'll find that they lose "steam" and importance once captured on paper. You have "said" them, and now, maybe you'll realize that they are better left there.

On good days, you can enter thoughts about great things you saw, heard, smelled, touched—people, places, things, and activities you liked. Suddenly, you have a treasure trove of stored happy stuff that you can go back to for inspiration. If you really enjoyed that cheeseburger and wrote about it, then when you turn back to your journal you may be inspired to pull out a cookbook and try to replicate that fabulous sandwich.

No one judges your journal, not even you. You can add art to it, keepsakes, doodles. Its whole purpose is to be your friend and companion. It's there when you want to say something. No pressure to write every day. You keep it to yourself, where others can't read it.

BARBARA ANN KIPFER

The process is what counts. Make the journaling process a personal, happy one for yourself.

26. Practice Daily Mindfulness

You can redefine *spiritual life* to be your day-to-day life, lived with intention and integrity. Every routine thing, from brushing your teeth to resolving a conflict to shoveling the snow, can be part of your spiritual practice. Instead of going through these things on automatic pilot, in an "impersonal" way, make your daily activities personal, really be there. Instead of feeling like you don't have time for spirituality, make the business of everyday living into a spiritual life.

Paying acute attention to each happening, each action, each word is called *mindfulness*. Each twenty-four-hour period is a gift of human life. Before, it often got away from you. Using mindfulness, none of it will get away from you—but it takes practice. It's so easy to go on autopilot. Plus, you think autopilot saves you time, but that is simply not true. Because you are not "in the moment," you often forget things, bobble things, and do other things that actually cost you time. And because you were not "in the moment," you actually threw that time away.

As you practice mindfulness during everyday activities, you will breathe more deeply and see more wonders. You will likely become more insightful, more content, and maybe more trusting. Practicing mindfulness of the body, feelings, mind, and mental objects when you do ordinary things like walk, drive, work, care for others, or do the most mundane things can be a new challenge. When you pay attention and become mindful, you marvel at the simple things in

30

life that you once passed over. These ordinary things are part of the journey of life, and you will find added happiness when you practice mindfulness every day.

27. Garden or Dig

Gardening and other digging is worth considering because it puts you back in touch with the earth and is a mind-body experience. Digging and gardening are humbling, as you are in the dirt, usually with insects and other funky stuff. You can garden in a backyard, a small plot, a window box—whatever you can work out. Another type of digging is volunteer archaeological fieldwork, which happens in most states under the direction of the state archaeologist.

Whether you choose gardening or another type of digging, you will also connect with the child in you. Most children love to play in a sandbox or at the beach or in dirt, just digging away and creating neat things. If you ever watch children in this type of environment, you will witness true joy and happiness. You may even remember the bliss you felt as a child when you did these activities. We can experience the same type of joy as adults; there are no age limits to gardening and digging.

Digging outside puts you in touch with Mother Nature, and allows you to connect with unfamiliar sounds, sights, and textures. It quiets your mind while you learn to labor. Whatever you plant will take time to grow and will require nurturing, so you also learn how to cultivate patience. Gardening and digging can be a way to get some important alone time, as well as exercise. This activity can easily become a healthy passion in your life.

The garden is a metaphor for sowing and reaping. Whatever you sow, you will reap. If you plant daisies, you will not get roses. If you sow positive seeds in your thoughts, deeds, and words, you will reap positive results.

A garden can teach you about miracles. A garden can be a reflection of you. Keep it simple and work with what is there—existing rocks, trees, bushes—and read up on what type of plants will likely flourish in this environment. Do everything you can to make this a fun process and experience.

28. Extricate Yourself from Technology and Noise

It is a whole different experience today when we lose electrical power due to a storm or other circumstance, compared to ten or twenty years ago. We have become so dependent on and indulgent of technology that when there is no telephone, television, or computer, we feel like a limb has been cut off. Some people have no idea what to do with themselves when this happens. Even though we appreciate what technology has offered in terms of advancements, it's still sad to realize that so much of our daily life is filled with technology and noise.

Everyday life is filled with computer sounds, the refrigerator humming, the dishwasher chugging, video-game songs and blips, the spinning of the washing machine, the thunking of the dryer; it goes on and on. The first step in extricating yourself from technology and noise is to become aware of how much of it is present in your life. When you become conscious of the amount, you will be a little surprised. It is very rare to hear complete silence or even the sounds of nature without the interference of electronic noise. We don't even realize how much irritability and irrationality is due to the assault on our brains by the sounds of technological life.

Scientists know that women are more sensitive to sounds. Our souls and minds crave peace and stillness. So, do turn off machines when you are not using them. Buy the quietest appliances you can, and avoid adding more gadgets like electric milkshake makers, citrus juicers, and can openers. There's nothing wrong with the manual version in most cases! Appreciate the simplicity and silence. Thrive on the new feelings you are experiencing.

You can do other things too: drive without the radio or other sounds; visit a park or walk in the woods and listen to the birds and other creatures; choose restaurants that don't overwhelm you with a soundtrack; watch television selectively, and don't leave it on for background noise; and add more music to your life. You will find that by embracing silence, a new sense of peace will enter your life.

29. Manage Your Time

You can stop your fight with time. There is plenty of time if you assume there is. And you can remind yourself that time is an arbitrarily imposed phenomenon; it is man-made. Time is defined as a continuum that lacks spatial dimensions. Time appears to be more puzzling than space because it seems to flow or pass by us, or else people seem to advance through it. But the passage of time seems to be unintelligible. Animals don't keep time, and scientists aren't even sure if they have a concept of time.

We give time too much power, and it intimidates us because we cannot create more. You can ease your struggle with time by learning time management skills. It's mainly about setting priorities and making the solid decision that you do indeed have time for what is important. You can say "no" to the extraneous, and learn how to graciously extract yourself from people and situations that should not take time away from you. There is an art to this process that will reap many rewards. People will learn to respect your honesty when you tell them that you just can't do something and give them a legitimate reason why. Don't make excuses. Just be honest, saying that you can only do so many things.

The process can be simple: You choose to do what matters first, and work from there. Learn to be positive about time instead of complaining about it. By reminding yourself why you are here—to delight in the present moment and the miracle of being alive—you can budget time for the important things. You can even learn to let go of your desire to impress others (by doing too much), and learn to do less instead.

Many people are afraid of empty time and fill it with television, talking, reading magazines—anything they can think of to avoid being "alone" with time. Very rarely do we stop doing things, be quiet, and pay attention. This is a serious problem. People don't feel comfortable just being with themselves and their thoughts, when this way of being should actually be encouraged and cherished. "Empty" time can become time for meditation, relaxation, and breathing—activities that will enrich our lives.

30. Write To-Do Lists and Notes

It is really important to write things down, to get into the practice of writing to-do notes or lists for yourself (and maybe for others), as well as asking others to write things down that they want you to do. Yes, slowing down and developing mindfulness and concentration helps us remember things better—but there's nothing like good, old-fashioned written notes to help you become more efficient in your daily life.

There's certainly enough paper and writing instruments in our homes and workplaces; we just need to distribute them in a smart way. A pad and pencil by the bedside, in the bathroom, in the kitchen, in a purse, even in the car—are all going to come in handy someday. A pad of Post-it notes works very well, allowing you to transfer the note to another spot without losing it.

There are countless "list people" out there (one survey says at least 42 percent of us keep to-do lists), and they all have a system they swear by. Some have an electronic grocery list they can print out for the refrigerator. Others keep a travel packing list or an entertaining/party list. Come birthday and holiday time, there are lists for gifts and cards. Written reminders do not indicate that we have a weak memory. They indicate that we care about carrying out small tasks efficiently and we take the time to note what we need or want to accomplish.

Many Web sites offer lists that you can adapt for your own needs. Lists keep you in the moment. They are tools for action and decision making. They reflect life as a work-in-progress. Maybe for you lists will become a way of life, a way of taking your pulse at any given moment. They do offer some feeling of control, but they can also be meditative. Most list makers agree that writing things down can have a magical effect of making things happen.

31. Forgetting the Right Things

Albert Schweitzer said, "Happiness? That's nothing more than health and a poor memory." He is on to something here. What good does it ever do to replay a conversation you wish had gone differently? Or replay an event that turned ugly? Yes, nostalgia for the good in the past can be heartwarming, but a lot of our ruminations about the past are not useful or good for us. Forgetting the right things can be healthy.

Enjoy your memory lapses. They are probably telling you something! Memory lapses make each moment a fresh experience. The most important moment is *now*. Live as if you won't remember tomorrow what you did today. Have a "beginner's mind," forgetting what you think you know and letting the world take you by surprise. What a refreshing way to live!

Forget what you want, but enjoy what you have. Forget to mention your accomplishments or possessions. You know what you have. Forget some bad things that were said to you or happened to you. It does no good to spend your precious time remembering them.

Take for granted that most people will forget what you said but will always remember how you made them feel. As for friends, the best ones do a lot of forgetting of those things that should be forgotten. And if you don't tell any lies, then you won't have to remember anything!

The concept of forgetting the things that should be forgotten adds happiness to your life. But the flip side is knowing what *not* to forget. Don't forget to look at the people you love and really appreciate them. Don't forget to pause often, slow down, be quiet, and pay attention. Don't forget your true friends, because a true friend stays true, no matter how much time goes by. Don't forget that you are in charge of creating your own happiness.

32. *Plan*

It helps to have goals. You can't leave it all to chance. You really should map out the foreseeable future, like the next one or two years, keeping in mind that life changes and your best-laid plans will sometimes conflict with uncontrollable fortune. Opportunity often knocks at an inopportune moment, but that doesn't mean you shouldn't set some goals.

To enjoy the present moment to the maximum, make a list of the things you would like to do in the next couple of years and put it on the wall by your desk. The longer the list, the better. Like this:

meditate every day
support public television
go on archaeology digs
eat only quality foods
keep a journal
read Rumi's poems
build the savings account

Over time, you will cross off some entries and add new ones, highlight others, and scribble notes everywhere. Decorate the area where you put this list, as it really is a shrine of the present and for the future as it unfolds. Just be prepared to improvise; the only thing that's certain is change! When you embrace change, you may be pleasantly surprised at some of the outcomes, because you'll be going *with* the flow instead of fighting it.

33. Accept Compliments and Gifts

No matter how caring you are, it is always a challenge to be on the receiving end of a compliment or gift. You can start by standing still while accepting a compliment, and making eye contact. Don't act embarrassed. Muster up dignity and accept graciously, honoring the feelings and judgment of your well-wisher. When it is your turn to give a compliment, you will know how to turn the occasion into a great moment.

With gifts, you must train yourself to open each one, big or small, with resolute conviction. Do not let anyone or anything distract you. Open it ceremoniously, carefully. Read the card out loud. Remove the ribbon and the wrapping paper, folding it and setting it aside. Simply saying "thank you" can often be the best way to receive a compliment or gift. The manner in which you receive a gift is a gift you can give in return.

You can extend this practice to accepting invitations and favors without feeling indebted as a result. You are paying your loved ones, friends, and acquaintances a great compliment by assuming that their largesse comes with no strings attached.

Guilt-free enjoyment of other people's kindness is a courageous act of faith. Trust that everyone out there is potentially as generous as you are.

Know the power of a generous heart, offer compliments, give accurate feedback, and listen carefully. You cannot lose by being generous. If you have a greedy thought, you can replace it with a generous one. Every day is filled with opportunities to be generous. When you give, give gracefully. When you present a gift or compliment to a person, also give your undivided attention.

34. Choose the More Demanding Option

Let's own up to the fact that labor-saving devices can often be time-consuming. Instead of making life easier, technology actually makes it shorter. Don't make your life easier, and you'll make it longer. To prolong the pleasure of being alive, do things that demand some effort on your part. Happiness comes not only from moment-to-moment enjoyment of life, but also from the sense of satisfaction that arises when you use your capacities to their fullest. Our bodies, minds, and spirits are made to be worked.

Sharpen pencils by hand, even with a knife. Take the stairs instead of the elevator. Make your own raspberry jam. Cook the entire Thanksgiving dinner (as opposed to heating it up). Spread your garden mulch yourself instead of hiring someone to do it. Walk to the store instead of driving there. Knit a sweater instead of purchasing one. Life feels a lot longer when you skip the shortcuts. Whenever you have a choice, choose the more demanding option.

This includes stretching yourself by learning, whether it's learning a new skill, pushing yourself to try a new sport, exploring new territory by traveling to a foreign country—this can be emotional or physical or mental or spiritual stretching. It's about reclaiming your time and life.

Look up that word in a print dictionary rather than typing it into a search engine. Before disagreeing with someone, try to walk a mile in the other person's shoes. Concentrate your efforts and use self-discipline to achieve that goal. Focusing your effort on the present, you will experience the spaciousness and ease of mind that comes from letting go of attachments. Enjoy the satisfaction that comes from effort.

35. *Find Serenity*

Taking pleasure in the simplest things brings serenity. Spiritual traditions and religions encourage believers to take part in rituals to explore the wonders of the ordinary: meditation in Buddhism; daily ablutions in Islam; processions and prayer in Christianity; the Japanese tea ceremony—to mention just a few. Small ceremonies and rituals infuse mundane activities with sacred meaning.

Rituals have "scripts" that free your mind for being in the moment. They are composed of simple gestures that keep the participants focused on the present moment: chanting, clapping, dancing, reciting, singing, walking, washing. Rituals let you experience tranquility and equanimity. Where can you add rituals to your daily life?

Serenity can be cultivated in other ways, too. If you are hoping for new ideas to come to you, looking for someone to date, trying to find someone in a crowd, or searching for something you lost—just stop and wait. Make yourself comfortable, make room in your mind, and listen. Suddenly, you are struck with a brilliant idea; your friend appears within the crowd, or you remember where you put that sweater. By being in the present moment, just being there, unperturbed, suspending the "quest," something will soon materialize—and maybe it will be exactly what you were looking for.

You can find a deep inner balance and serenity in the midst of all the commotion, through rituals and pauses. And there's always the Serenity Prayer:

God grant me the serenity
to accept the things I cannot change;
the courage to change the things I can;
and the wisdom to know the difference.
Living one day at a time;
enjoying one moment at a time;
accepting hardships as the pathway to peace;
taking, as He did, this sinful world
as it is, not as I would have it;
trusting that He will make all things right
if I surrender to His will;
that I may be reasonably happy in this life
and supremely happy with Him
forever in the next.
Amen.

36. Do One Thing at a Time

Remember the proverb your mother repeated: "One thing at a time, and that done well, is a very good thing, as many (or any) can tell"? Doing one thing at a time seems unusual in our multitasking world, even though we are all quite aware of the confusion and mistakes often caused by multitasking. It's like splitting our brain to do different things; reading the newspaper while eating breakfast is a good example. Are you really chewing well and tasting each bite? If you train yourself to *be aware* while you eat and read the newspaper, then it is more like doing one thing.

The days when you derived a lot of satisfaction from doing one thing at a time do not have to be in the past. You can revive this, if even in small gestures and rituals. When you brush your teeth, really *feel* the toothbrush on every tooth. When you fold the laundry, smooth and fold each item carefully. When you tie your shoes, look at the knot as you create it. Being aware of doing one thing at a time is a very comforting experience. You will find that as you do one thing at a time more often, you will feel more confident completing things that are more complicated.

Also, productivity isn't just about getting through a task—it should also be about completing the task with some level of quality. Rushing through a task quickly to declare it's "complete" isn't productivity, since if it isn't done well, someone (probably you) will just have to clean it up later. The fact is, most people aren't getting much done and are not experiencing the satisfaction of completing each task—especially not with any quality or thought—because we are all too busy multitasking.

The human brain just isn't meant to take on more than one or two tasks at a time, and the level of attentiveness to quality breaks down quickly as more distractions pile up. Aim and sustain your attention, and focus on one thing at a time.

37. Give Thanks

Embrace gratitude and saying "thank you," and you will see great benefits in your life. Giving thanks is an important dimension as we interact with one another in our everyday lives. We are all connected, and being grateful for our blessings—for those who do well by us, for every little thing (even hardships that teach us life lessons)— makes us healthier and happier.

You may not even be aware of the miracle of your very existence as a human being, or the astronomical odds that surround anything happening at a given time and place. You are a lucky accident, and for that alone you should be grateful.

Think of the gifts you have received from your ancestors and parents, from friends, loved ones, partners, and colleagues. It is a privilege to know them and be part of their lives. Without them and their tempering influence on your mind's delusions and illusions, who knows where you would be today? Give thanks for all that you have received and your life will be much richer.

Albert Einstein said that he had to remind himself a thousand times a day of how much he depended upon other people. Even if there are times when you have trouble being grateful for family, friends, and loved ones, you need to acknowledge that there's a whole world of people out there who make your life possible.

Remind yourself to be grateful to them, too. Gratitude requires work, but it is important work, and every effort should be made to cultivate it. Cultivate generosity, gratitude, and kindness for even the smallest joys and wonders.

38. Practice Basic Meditation

The purpose of meditation is to calm the mind, cultivating awareness and attention. The main theme is simplicity, going back to your most natural state. The following basic meditation is a great way to start.

- *Sit comfortably (in whatever position that is for you), and let your eyes close gently.*
- *Invite your body to relax and release into the ground or cushion.*
- *Let go and accept the non-doing of meditation.*
- *Become sensitive to and listen to your breath. Breathe through your nose. Feel the air as it goes in and out of the nostrils. Feel the rising and falling of the chest and abdomen. Allow your attention to settle where you feel the breath most clearly. Focus there.*
- *Follow the breath. Allow the breath to be as it is without controlling it. See the space or pause between breaths.*
- *Thinking will start. It is a habit. See each thought like a railroad car of a train going by. See it, acknowledge it, let it go, and come back to the breath.*
- *It does not matter how many times you get caught up in a thought or for how long. Begin again and bring awareness*

back to the breath. This is your practice. You are strengthening
mindfulness.

- *Awareness of one whole in-breath and one whole out-breath is
a big accomplishment.*
- *If a physical sensation or pain arises, do the same. See it,
acknowledge it without getting caught up by it, let it go, and
come back to the breath.*
- *For twenty minutes, follow your breath with total attention.
When your mind wanders, stop and come back to the breath.
As you gently open your eyes, try to carry the momentum of
your mindfulness into whatever your next activity may be.*

39. Lounge

**The art of doing nothing (without feeling guilty) has to be relearned
by many of us.** At the end of the day, it is important to take your
mind off of things and let your thoughts idle. Your cognitive self
needs to slow down before you can get a good night's sleep. You
can lounge alone or with others. You get into a comfortable position
and stay put until your brain settles.

Lounging can be done in a chaise lounge, on a couch, on a porch
swing, in a hammock, in a beanbag chair, in a nice warm bath, etc.
My favorite spot is a special wing chair I have in our bedroom.
It's about savoring silence, but it does require patience. You drop
anchor and just rest. The process requires you to be aware that
the lounging is beginning. Experience the initial feelings and look
forward to it continuing.

No matter what calls to you—something you forgot to fix, the
phone, the pull to write down a list on a Post-it note—you just stay
put. You are restless and it takes time to quiet down your mental

activity and manage your restlessness. Put your conscious mind on sabbatical.

Stay prone as long as you can, reclining, with your center of gravity close to the floor. It certainly is possible to get a brilliant idea while floating in a bubble bath!

40. Practice Reflexology

Through your feet, you channel excess energy into the earth. How good does it feel to kick off your shoes in the evening (or on an airplane or under a restaurant table)? With that move, you reestablish direct contact with the ground and release tensions.

Reflexology is an ancient Chinese healing technique, a form of alternative medicine used to restore the flow of energy in the body by massaging specific points on the feet, but also on the hands and ears. Each of the "reflex points" relates to specific organs and glands in the body. Practitioners believe that stimulating those reflex points promotes health in that organ via the body's energetic pathways. There are many books available to help you learn the technique; you can even buy socks that have the reflex points marked on them.

Reflexology is a great activity to perform with a partner or practitioner, but even doing your own foot massage will help. You massage the balls of the feet, between the toes, across the arch, up the tendons on the back of the foot. The ankles can be circled, toes wiggled. Even standing up, you can perform a little massage by gently pushing against the floor with different parts of the feet: arches, heels, toes.

Reflexology can be a good treatment choice for people who want to keep their clothes on during a massage. It is also a good choice if you are pressed for time and don't want to get oil on your body or in your hair. The benefits are instantaneous.

41. Take a Nap

Taking naps can change your life. Sometimes curling up on a couch for just ten minutes is the best way to revive yourself, increasing your alertness, boosting creativity, and reducing stress. Naps will also improve perception, stamina, motor skills, and accuracy; enhance your sex life; help you make better decisions; keep you looking younger; aid in weight loss; reduce the risk of heart attack; elevate your mood; and strengthen memory. Wow! In many cultures, napping is an accepted part of the day and a natural thing to do.

It is an art to learn when, where, and for how long to nap. Until you get the hang of what is right for you, you may find you wake up cranky or groggy. But if you keep trying, you will find the right combination. The urge to take a nap is usually the best guidance. There are even books with guidance on how to assess your tiredness, set up a personal sleep profile, and neutralize the voice in your head that tells you napping is a sign of laziness. Napping is definitely not a sign of laziness. In fact, once you master the art of napping, you will notice that you are able to get more done and be in a better mood.

Even at work, napping is becoming an accepted activity. At the office, this might mean closing the door and laying your head on your desk, or even curling up on the floor. Even at home you have to get creative to avoid being awakened by a phone or another person. You can glance at the clock and set in your mind how long you want to nap, then trust your subconscious to nudge you when it is time to wake up (or you can set an alarm).

Don't hurtle yourself back into activity. Pull yourself out slowly, like dragging a boat onto the beach. Stretch, maybe wash your face and hands. Surrendering to a nap does more than just restore the ability to function efficiently. It actually generates a clear and transparent state of mind, making you more awake and aware of what's around you.

42. Sit Still

Your mind swings like a monkey from tree to tree, thought to thought. Most people aren't calmly aware, like cats; they are more like undomesticated animals, high-strung and easily spooked. Mindfulness and meditation practices help you learn to sit still and explore the territory of your big mind, to find the calm center that exists in you. Sitting still is not as easy as it sounds, and it does take practice, but it's a skill well worth cultivating.

The first step is to establish contact with the ground. You invite your body to relax and release into the ground (or cushion or chair). Mentally, you connect the top of your head with your right foot, then the top of your head with your left foot. You mentally tether these points of your body and let your hands gently drape one over the other, or one on each knee. You think of the head as reaching up, so that your body does not go slack. It is also important to be aware of your breathing. Make sure your breathing is rhythmic and deep.

There's your mind. Thinking will start. It is a habit. See each thought as a railroad car jumbling by. You see it, then let it pass out of view. The hard part is letting each thought go. It's important to not hang on to one, thinking more about it or judging it. Just let it keep going by.

This is something you start over and over again, even during a five-minute or twenty-minute sitting. That's why it is called practice. See every thought or sensation, acknowledge it without getting caught up by it, let it go, and come back to the breath. The true benefit of sitting still is when you are able to carry over this mindfulness into your other daily activities.

43. Steam Your Face

A hot face steaming is a forgotten home remedy that is great for the common cold, for ridding the body of toxins, and for preparing for a lovely night's sleep. It's also yummy in the middle of winter for warming yourself in a delicious way. Face steaming is an affordable luxury that will increase your feeling of happiness.

Allow about twenty minutes for face steaming. If you can, put a chair in front of your sink and put a pillow or two on the seat so you can sit similarly to sitting at a desk. This can even be done at the bathtub, although that will require a lot more water. Tie your hair up, get into pajamas, and roll up the sleeves. No glasses or contact lenses, please. Fill the basin with hot water. If you'd like, you can add scented bath oils, such as lavender.

Start with a clean face. Cover your head with a clean towel and cross your arms in front of you, submerging them in the hot water for maximum effect. Every five minutes, add more hot water. The steam releases sweat and toxins from every pore.

At the end of twenty minutes, rinse your face with lukewarm water, dry off, and go straight to bed. You should sleep wonderfully and awaken with lots of energy.

44. Savor Food and Drink

To eat in a mindful way, every bite and crumb should be fully and completely tasted. If you are present in your eating, you can't binge. You may find more enjoyment in healthful foods. If you savor every bite of chocolate or french fries, you won't need much. Though we eat to nourish our bodies, we taste food to satiate our minds. The brain feasts on the aroma and flavor of each mindful bite and sip we bring to our mouths, long before the stomach is part of the process.

Eating mindfully requires great concentration. Think of how many times you've spent an hour preparing a dinner that everyone ate in five minutes! Sad! There are more than five million smell- and taste-sensing cells in our body. Flavor is wrapped up in color, shape, sound, temperature, and texture. Marcel Proust demonstrated this to the world with his story of the madeleine cake. In his novel, *Swann's Way*, the narrator experiences an awakening upon truly and thoroughly tasting a madeleine cake. You can understand how savoring food and drink is an entirely different, and happier, experience than gulping something down without taking the time to explore all of its features.

When you eat or drink something, take it in with your eyes and nose before starting. We have talked about eating quality food, but even that is not as satisfying if you don't savor it. Take a small bite or sip and move it around in your mouth. Wine tasters do this to fully experience the wine. Put the utensil or glass down. Sense what type of taste it is. Fully chew if it is food and then enjoy the swallow. Notice the impulse to take another bite before the first is chewed and swallowed. *Be* with every aspect of this experience. Give thanks for this first taste and those to come. Continue to eat and drink with mindfulness, as slowly as you can.

45. Listen and Seek Silence

We seem to crave talking; we can't get enough of it. In many cases we talk just to hear ourselves speak. Shouldn't we do an equal amount of listening, and also, seek more silence? The ability to speak and write is unique to humans, and we can cultivate this miracle in much more mindful ways.

Our brains constantly pick up all types of information, even from nonverbal clues. We often finish other people's sentences. We can read the lips of people on television and across the room. But a major portion of what we think we just heard is the product of our imagination. Without realizing it, we fill in the gaps in other people's utterances, even going so far as to correct their grammar, add punctuation, substitute words, and interpret accents—re-creating their speech even as they are offering it.

But in doing this, you are not truly listening. We need to be clearer about the boundaries between speaking and listening. When practicing mindful listening, give others your full attention. Relax. Let yourself open up to the words that are coming toward you. Concentrate on every word that they say. Try to understand the meaning of the words that are being spoken. You don't have to actively participate; just look, smile, nod—whatever is appropriate. The more you listen to others, the more they will listen to you. By becoming a mindful listener and focusing on what others are saying, you will find that your communications are much happier.

But also remember that silence is golden. If you don't constantly talk about your favorite subject, it will stay your favorite subject. Not bragging or seeking recognition will ensure that you do not become complacent and will endear you to others. Not saying anything when you have nothing to say will prove you wise. And not saying anything unless you have something useful and kind to say is the best advice of all.

46. Wait in the Moment

We tend to think a lot about the future, and while goals are necessary and healthy, a focus on what's next often causes us to miss out on the *now*. Anything you can do to become less obsessed with what is going to happen next gives you more room to stay in the present moment, which is one of the key elements to happiness.

Waiting is hard when we haven't learned to stay with the now. So often we are thinking about the past or the future, or wishing that the present moment was something other than what it is. You can change the way you feel about waiting by using the correct tense when you are stuck in a waiting situation. By following a few simple steps, more reminders than anything, you will transform yourself to be in the present moment. Be positive. Say, "My plane will leave in two hours," and give yourself two hours of free time instead of two hours spent waiting for your flight to leave. Taking the time to wait, being in the present, is not a waste.

Waiting is the practice of patience. You develop your ability to wait and to listen by going deep into stillness. Deep, slow breaths help you practice waiting in the present moment. Do mindful waiting. Use the opportunity to create a sacred moment. Breathe in and out three times, refreshing yourself through awareness.

We are always in the midst of exciting and uncertain times, filled with much anticipation and frustration; what better way to endure the wait than to sit back, treasure each day for its own merits, and enjoy the wait.

47. Take Pictures with Your Mind

Though we usually take pictures to capture a special occasion, we can also fix an impression forever in our memories by closing our eyes and savoring the moment with our other senses. Pay close attention to momentary pleasures and wonders. Focus on the sweetness of a ripe strawberry, or the warmth of the sun when you step out from the shade. Some psychologists suggest taking "mental photographs" of pleasurable moments to relive in less happy times. Some philosophers even argue that mental photographs are more accurate than physical ones! The mind can recognize or use the relevant aspects of resemblance between a photograph (or an inner quasi picture) and an object (or a percept), so the mind must already be able to represent the picture and its object, and their various features, to itself.

A slightly different take on this is to read a list of happy things, as found on www.thingstobehappyabout.com, and you will see all kinds of mental pictures of the things that are meaningful to you. You will find this to be a very pleasing activity that generates happiness.

48. Mute Your Mind

That running commentary in your head is something you can do without. You go over and over things that were said in the past, rehearse over and over the things you want to say in the future. Your mind keeps this commentary going, almost in hopes that the thoughts will become reality. This is unhealthy. We are not our thoughts, and finding a way to mute your mind is going to bring you some peace.

Meditation is one way to more accurately understand this commentary. Being able to recognize the chatter is the first step toward muting the thoughts. You know that songs often get "stuck" in your head, too, and when you recognize one and say, "Halt!", it often works to stop the music.

Part of why some people are afraid of silence is because then they are faced with the incessant chatter of their minds. Instead of avoiding this by talking or watching television or doing other mindless activities, why not try a type of meditation to find a way to mute the thoughts and find a calmness in quiet moments?

Very rarely do we stop doing things, be quiet, and pay attention. Create a mental off button that will bring peace and quiet. Only a quiet and receptive mind can learn. Aim to learn a natural quietness of mind and openness of heart. The quieter you become, the more you will hear.

49. Be Ordinary

You would not know this from reading *In Style* or *People* magazines, but being ordinary is perfect. The only difference between an extraordinary life and an ordinary one is the extraordinary pleasures you find in ordinary things.

Remind yourself of your ordinariness on a regular basis. It's good for your character. You don't need to save your junk for posterity. You probably don't need to spend money on therapy. There is great satisfaction in little things, like feeding the cat. You can be late and the sky won't fall. You can miss a day of work and the world will not end. You don't have to travel the world to search for something you have right at home. No one notices if your socks match your outfit perfectly, whether your car is clean, or what you are wearing when you shoot out to the store for milk. Be content to be nobody special. Exult in being ordinary.

The charm of Ziggy, the comic book character, is that he lives a sweetly simple life. Things often don't go his way, but he always perseveres and maintains his sunny outlook. Ziggy is Everyperson, the part of us that harbors warm feelings and good intentions but sometimes gets stepped on by a reckless world. Ziggy exhibits steadfastness, tenacity, and a gentle spirit.

Why do so many people identify with Ziggy? Because he represents the innocent side found in everyone, the optimist who lives deep down and wants to see the good in everything. No matter how bad things get, Ziggy always finds the bright spot. He finds it easier to relate to his animal friends than to people, and he often contemplates the meaning of life with his accepting pets. His insecurities encourage us to laugh at ourselves and to take everything in stride. Ziggy is about seeing the world with some humor and following your dreams no matter what. Be humble like Ziggy! Ordinary is perfect.

50. Let Go of Unneeded Items

Men laugh at this, but women totally appreciate that throwing away or giving away old things is a new beginning. Some things may be kept for the sake of nostalgia, but there is really no need to hold on to what is obsolete. Sure, you may suddenly ask "Where is the potato ricer?" a couple of weeks after you've thrown it out, but then you will laugh. You don't really need it.

For every object we cast off, we have our memories. These impressions are things you can write down or just put in your memory bank. It's all about trading impermanent objects for permanent recollections. We have to be willing to let go.

One really great exercise is to find at least one thing each week to either donate, throw away, or consign. Maybe the number will change, but clearing clutter is invigorating. If you give things away so others may benefit, it is satisfying; if you sell items you no longer use or need, your wallet benefits, and that is satisfying, too. Just make sure that the reason you're clearing things out is not because you plan to turn around and buy new stuff to take its place!

Excess clothing? Tired knickknacks? Books no one intends to read? Letting go of unneeded items can keep you in the present moment and free you from attachments. It feels *so* good.

51. Keep the Mind in Good Working Order

Are you getting forgetful or having trouble learning new things? There are simple exercises you can do to stimulate the production of nutrients that grow brain cells to keep the brain younger and stronger. You can whip your neurological pathways into good working order, mainly by inventing new ways to think about the same old things. This creates new connections between existing neurons so the brain can maintain, repair, and regenerate itself.

Doing crossword puzzles or Sudoku, learning a new word a day, writing in a journal, playing word association games, taking quizzes, taking part in trivia games—these are just a few of the possibilities. The requirements for an activity that will work on your mind in this way include the following:

- *The activity must involve one or more of your senses in a new context, like eating a meal with your family in silence, or combine two or more senses in unexpected ways, like listening to a specific piece of music while smelling a particular aroma.*
- *The activity must engage your attention, like taking your child to the office with you for a day or trying to answer timed questions in a math game.*

• *The activity must be a break from routine, like taking a completely new route to work or shopping at a farmers' market instead of a supermarket.*

When I take a hike in the woods by our house, I usually follow the same route each time. But once in a while, I reverse the route, which forces me to concentrate in order to stay on that path. The things that I have seen over and over again look different and new. It is very invigorating and challenging and helps me keep my mind in good working order.

You'll find many resources out there to help you jump-start your brain-building activities, like Lawrence Katz's book, *Keep Your Brain Alive*, and even video games like *Brain Age* (Nintendo).

52. Laugh

First of all, we need to have a sense of humor about ourselves. If we can't laugh at ourselves, especially when we take ourselves too seriously, what can we laugh at? The sudden deflation of our ego triggers a moment of levity.

Zen practitioners often participate in laughing out loud. Many people might be surprised to think of laughter as a form of meditation. Yet not only is laughing meditation one of the simplest forms of meditation, it is also a very powerful one. The physical act of laughing is one of the few actions that involve the body, the emotions, and the soul. When we laugh, we give ourselves over to the immediacy of the present moment. We are also able to momentarily transcend minor physical and mental stresses. Practiced in the morning, laughing meditation can lend a joyful quality to the entire day. Practiced in the evening, laughing meditation is a potent relaxant that has been known to inspire pleasant dreams. Laughter can also help open our eyes to previously unnoticed absurdities that can make life seem less serious.

There are three stages to mindful laughter, and each one can last anywhere from five to twenty minutes. The first stage involves stretching your body like a cat and breathing deeply. Your stretch should start at the hands and feet before you move through the rest of your body. Stretch out the muscles in your face by yawning and making silly faces. The second stage of the meditation is pure laughter. Imagine a humorous situation, remember funny jokes, or think about how odd it is to be laughing by yourself. When the giggles start to rise, let them. Let the laughter ripple through your belly and down into the soles of your feet. Let the laughter lead to physical movement. Roll on the floor, if you have to, and keep on laughing until you stop. The final stage of the meditation is one of silence. Sit with your eyes closed and focus on your breath.

Laughter brings with it a host of positive effects that operate on both the physical and mental levels. It is also fun, expressive, and a way to release tension. Learn to laugh in the present moment, and you'll find that joy is always there. Keep in mind how good you feel after an uncontrollable laughing attack!

53. Seek Moments

What is missing from many of our days is the sense that we are truly enjoying the lives we are living. To experience moments of happiness, we have to be aware of what we genuinely love. Many people think that they can only be happy on the weekends or when they retire. They wait for those times to feel happy. How many happy moments are missed because our focus is on something big that may happen in the future, and not our simple, day-to-day pleasures? We must learn to seek out and savor moments that bring us contentment and joy.

Some things you try may seem indulgent at first, but what are you waiting for? Don't you deserve happiness right now? What if you took the time to carefully arrange some fresh flowers, or drank your cup of coffee in the sun on the porch? What if you stopped for five minutes to pet a purring cat? Putting simple pleasures into your life and appreciating ones that just happen really bring happiness to your day.

Only you can make yourself aware of what makes you happy. It is a good exercise to write down your personal preferences and delights so you can learn how to generate, recognize, and embrace these joyful moments.

> Happiness is not a brilliant climax to years of grim struggle and anxiety. It is a long succession of little decisions simply to be happy in the moment.
>
> —J. Donald Walters

54. Pay Attention

Things leap out at me, especially off the printed page. I pick up a book or a magazine, and a sentence or phrase leaps off the page as if it had been written just for me. Or I hear a revelation in the lyrics of a song, or even in the lines of an advertisement. I write all these things down on my list, which gets transferred to my database, which now has more than 100,000 things to be happy about.

Once I started this list in sixth grade, my list grew. It made every day worthwhile, picking up just a few things a day to add to the list. When I look back at this "paying attention to life," I feel rich. I experienced every day and made note of it. Really, it is all about paying attention. I cultivated my mind's natural capacity for concentration. This capacity reveals itself all the time in daily life.

When I see a tiny red granite rock on my walk, I am fascinated by its color and shape. My attention sinks into the rock as I examine it. The rock holds my attention for a couple of delightful minutes. Brain waves lengthen, feelings of oneness with the object arise, a peaceful and calm mind state emerges. These experiences happen to us more frequently than we think. At the symphony, the mind gets locked onto a beautiful violin line in a Bach concerto. At dinner, we find a morsel of food particularly remarkable. Both of these experiences involve a natural emergence of singular attention.

If you read a lot, it's a gratifying exercise to keep a notebook nearby and jot down the things that strike you. There's no right or wrong way to do it; it's whatever makes you feel good when you read it. Your observations of life can be captured one at a time and gathered in a notebook, ready to be glanced at when you're feeling down (or simply when you want a great idea for dinner).

55. Create a Gratitude Journal

Writing in a journal is a very personal thing to do. There are many forms of journaling, here are a few:

- *the old-fashioned diary*
- *a list of things to be happy about (my favorite type of journal)*
- *art journal*
- *gratitude journal*

All of these tools for inner exploration can help you become happier and more content, and will also nurture your creativity.

A daily gratitude journal consists of writing down five things every evening that you are grateful for from the day. Sometimes you will have amazing things to be grateful for, and other times you may struggle to find the five things and start writing entries that seem very simplistic to you. Again, there is no right or wrong way to do this type of journal. There are bad days, depressing times, when just saying you are grateful for your husband, your pet, your home is all you can muster. That's okay; writing these down helps, too.

Gratitude is essential to transform your path to happiness. It is important to give thanks each day for the abundance that exists in your life. The more you are grateful, the more you will have to be grateful about. It's a process that feeds itself, and it's really quite simple. All you need is the most wonderful blank book you can find (and there are many kinds to choose from these days) and your favorite writing instrument.

After a while, you will look forward to adding to this each day. And your days will be changed by your inner shift toward looking for more things to be grateful for. You will seek out the positive, the optimistic, the wonders in the every day. And telling people you are grateful to have them in your life, for what they have done, for who they are, is a very powerful expression of caring and love. Telling a stranger who has given you something (directions, good service, a smile) that you are grateful is another form of connection. Spread the idea of gratitude.

56. Find Beauty

Some days it's possible to see much more beauty in the world than on others. It's easy to find beauty on a sunny day with blue skies, when many things look attractive. The trick then becomes learning how to stretch and recognize beauty even on the crappiest days.

Maybe you do this by having some coffee-table or art books to peruse. Just one or two that have pictures that speak to you will do the trick. Or you could visit an art gallery or museum on your lunch hour, or just after work. If you have a favorite painting at home, you could meditate on it. Looking at plants and flowers is also a great way to find beauty. And, finally, there are the faces of your loved ones—a beautiful sight anytime.

Much has been written about making your home comfortable and beautiful, within your budget. Too much focus on decorating is unhealthy, especially if you spend time and money thinking that the new things, or the new look, will bring you happiness. The reality is that the newness wears off and the bill still has to be paid.

You should be able to furnish and decorate your home and then appreciate it that way for some time. Having lit candles on the dinner table is an example of something affordable you can do to really warm and beautify the meal.

Sometimes the tiniest things are the most fascinating. You will get a lot of joy from an inexpensive microscope with which you can view mounted specimens on slides. A magnifying glass works well, too. And to enjoy the little things outdoors, just grab some binoculars or your child's telescope. There's more beauty out there than what meets the naked eye.

57. Have Inner Dialogue

We talk to ourselves all the time—don't deny it! Sometimes it's great when everyone is out of the house and we can actually sit and talk to ourselves out loud. I know I have worked through some tough feelings that way. I know that it would look funny if anyone saw me doing this, but I can't deny how much it has helped at times.

Instead of keeping a diary, I sensed that making a happiness list was better for me, and I started one in the sixth grade. At first I just recorded simple stuff, like "blueberry muffins." I gradually expanded and enhanced my list, which now includes more than 100,000 items.

I also followed a wonderful system set up by Ira Progoff in his book, *At a Journal Workshop*. His program offers more than a chronological diary; the Intensive Journal Process is a complex and systematic method for gaining self-insight by recording thoughts, dreams, and significant events, which are then used as focal points for meditation and written reflection in separate sections.

But you can do this on your own quite simply: Take a notebook and have a conversation with yourself on paper. Everything you are worried about can just spill out into the notebook as a stream of consciousness. You download what's going on in your brain to the paper, which will have a cleansing effect. You will become more centered, more energetic, more creative. It is quite therapeutic.

If you like this activity, try writing a daily dialogue for twenty-one days, the length of time psychologists say is required for a new behavior to become a habit. The amount of time you spend or the number of pages you write doesn't matter—just the consistency of writing every day for twenty-one days. It is a self-nurturing ritual with a reassuring rhythm, and you may find that you're able to resolve many issues by laying down all your worries, complaints, and fears in that notebook. (You should use just a plain notebook for this exercise, not a pretty journal. This is just a place to dump everything!)

58. Keep an Illustrated Journal

There are plenty of artists out there who would much rather create an illustrated journal or simply annotate their own sketchbook. Art journals live in the pockets and purses and backpacks of all kinds of artists. A birder on a morning walk, a scientist in the field, a film director delayed in a foreign airport, a fashion designer musing over next season's collection, a teenager avoiding schoolwork—all keep journals that serve as confidants and/or workhorses. Like a handmade quilt, an illustrated journal is transformed by holding within it the life created by the journal keeper.

In her essay, "On Keeping a Notebook," Joan Didion says that a journal is of no use to anyone except its keeper. Didion says, "We forget all too soon the things we thought we could never forget." Visual or illustrated journals become like explorers' logs, where you feed the imagination by gathering beautiful images that speak to your soul. The quality of the artwork is not the important element in this exercise. The process that you go through is what leads to growth.

You can draw or paint in your journal. You can cut out pictures from magazines and glue them in. You can collage. Then you might want to add quotes, greeting cards, art postcards, beautiful pieces of wrapping paper, or origami paper. As with other types of journals, there are no hard-and-fast rules.

The visual journal sheds light on the author's complex creative process. Artists' books, travel journals, and scientists' field books all have different focuses, but all are about *observation*—being awake and aware in the world. Observation then becomes reflection in these journals of exploration and creation. Journals of exploration may be literal or figurative, but, either way, they help the author to look outside his or her usual confines and revive the senses. Journals of creation are tangles of realized ideas. The illustrated journal is both personal and pragmatic, an account of times spent observing and recording what so many of us never notice. Great wisdom comes from looking closely at our world.

59. Find a Favorite Pastime

An oft-shared piece of advice is to find pastimes that make you happy. This is not as easy as it sounds. We often feel guilty if we choose to do a creative endeavor on our own. Many of us do not allow ourselves this type of "indulgence." There is always a reason not to, like a spouse, children, elderly parents, our career, money, time, etc. You get the point.

What we fail to realize is that everyone around us benefits if we are happy. So put away the excuses and start searching for your favorite pastime.

- *take an art course*
- *join a knitting group*
- *become part of a Wednesday-matinee movie club*
- *sign up for that cooking class*
- *play golf*
- *take a nice hike*
- *take yourself out for a meal once a week, all by yourself*
- *go to a bookstore to browse after work or on the weekend*

A favorite pastime is not judged by how much money it costs, how much time it takes, or how much you can talk about it with other people; it is judged by your heart. When you embark on a creative journey that fulfills you, your heart sings. I cannot emphasize this enough: Do not listen to excuses or feel guilty for pursuing your pastime. Do not give up! You can make the time and find the support that will allow you to do it.

Once you realize that nurturing yourself makes you happy, you will notice that it makes those around you feel good, too. So, don't put it off. Choose an activity and get started. As you take this first step, with gratitude, you walk in liberation.

60. Create a Happy List

You should know what makes you happy. But maybe you just do so many other things, you don't take the time to think about it. Beginning a happy list will make you think about it. It will give you the tool you need to start defining what truly makes you happy. I'm begging you to start.

I can't think of a better way than to grab a little notebook and write down one, two, three, four, or five things that made you happy today. These should be word pictures. Words, and the images they create, can be a great source of pleasure and inspiration. Sometimes, on a gray day, I flip through my collection to cheer myself up or remind myself to be grateful; often I use it to get ideas about what to cook for dinner or something fun to do on the weekend. Conjure up your own images and collect them to help you reminisce, wish, and dream. As your happy list grows over time, it will become a time capsule of what has made you happy throughout your life. What a great feeling, to reflect on all of the happy things you've experienced over the years!

Sometimes I write something down that personally I don't really like ("the way peanut butter spreads"). Even though I have to hold my nose when doing it (because, to me, it is one of the worst smells on Earth), I still get a kick out of the way peanut butter spreads when I'm making a peanut butter and jelly sandwich for my son.

Do you get the idea? You're creating a unique list of word pictures that either brings happiness to you, or to someone else, and capturing it on paper. Your list says so much about you, and allows you to focus on the things that make you happy. This is truly an important step on your pathway toward happiness.

61. Go On a Media Diet

The world can become too much at times. When you stop to think about it, we live in a pretty crazy world. Why make it worse by watching television news or reading the newspaper? The assault on the senses from the media is often the last straw. When we eat too much, we often cut back. When we feel overwhelmed by the state of the world, why not cut back on our media intake? Do you honestly think you will miss it? If something major happens, you'll hear about it.

How about curtailing the amount of time spent listening to iPods or car radios? No chatting on cell phones. No surfing Web sites or watching television. The art of alone time is increasingly lost in our hectic, frazzled, wired lives. Going on a media diet is an experiment in restorative solitude that explores the importance of quiet time for clarity, creativity, and spirituality.

Before you go on the diet, you could log your consumption for a few days—just to give yourself an idea of what you have been doing, how much time has been involved, and to jump-start the experiment. The media diet will likely come as a revelation to you.

The silence will be deafening. You have to get comfortable with just listening to yourself and your thoughts, because there's nothing else to distract you. Meditation certainly helps with that. As the diet proceeds and you become more comfortable, you will see benefits, like being better able to concentrate and having more free time to spend doing things you love.

Be aware in the future that what you take in from the media affects your karma, your destiny or condition in this life. Choose carefully, trying not to fill your mind with harmful or disturbing information.

62. Do Something New

Most of us feel more secure when we play it safe. We become comfortable with the tried and true and are often afraid to try something new. Yet every day we have chances to embrace the new. It could be serving something different with hamburgers than the usual french fries. It could be wearing comfy shoes instead of a highly fashionable pair. It could be pulling your hair back with a headband instead of barrettes.

Doing something new or taking a little risk each day makes you feel great once you have done it. Then you can think about taking bigger risks that will bring even more happiness. You might be afraid of taking up a new type of exercise or changing careers or going back to school. Prepare for these bigger risks by starting off with small things.

Each time you experience something new, you become receptive to inspiration. Each time you try something new, you empower yourself. Break down the walls that you have put up your entire life. Respect these creative urges, and you will discover that your choices are more meaningful to you. I love hearing stories about people who have tried something new and have changed their whole lives for the better because of it. Become one of those stories. Try something new.

With awareness, you feel creative, you discover new solutions to problems, and you are better able to maintain your balance and perspective in trying circumstances.

63. Meditate on Present Moment

See the perfectness of the present moment in every ordinary moment, in every difficult moment, in every good moment. Appreciate, respond, and sense the "bloom" of each moment. Dwelling in the present, know that this is a wonderful moment.

Bring yourself back into the present moment by becoming mindful of objects and events that are arising. Know you are breathing in. Know you are breathing out. Be aware of the hair on your head. Be aware of the soles of your feet. Dwell in the present moment. Be aware this is the only moment when you are alive.

Be aware of the space between the thoughts in your mind. Be aware that you are not caught up in thinking. Feel calm and stable. Dwell in the present moment.

When you are standing there, impatiently trying to get the toaster to work faster, wake up! Breathe, smile, and settle into the present moment. Create a "stop-sign practice" out of this type of experience. During the three minutes that the toaster is doing its thing, just breathe and calm yourself. Waiting for the toast is an opportunity for you to experience peace. Become aware of other opportunities that arise for you to meditate on the present moment. The more you practice it, the better you will get. You will reach a point where you love being in each and every moment.

64. *Keep a Comfort Drawer*

A comfort drawer is for times like those nights when you just want to crawl into bed, pull the blankets over you, and not come out. Whether it is a big thing, small thing, or a combination of things that have happened to make you feel this way, your comfort drawer is there for you. Everyone has been there at some time in his or her life. You can stockpile small indulgences in a drawer and dip into it when you come up against one of these times.

Your comfort drawer could contain:

magazines
an herbal eye pillow
wrapped candies or chocolate
a rejuvenating essential oil, like ylang-ylang
a scrapbook
a favorite paperback or book of quotes
a special candle
a CD for meditation
a "happy list" notebook

The comfort drawer is all about pampering yourself. It should be pretty and inspiring inside, too, so you feel like you are opening a present. There is nothing wrong with having something be all about pleasure, as long as you are aware of that.

The comfort drawer is full of goodies that you turn to only when you've had it. You can build it up as certain items go on sale, or ask for stocking stuffers or birthday treats that you can save for a yucky day. Part of the appeal of a comfort drawer is filling it. By taking pride in the preparation, you assure yourself of some comfort when you need it the most.

65. Remove the Blues

Getting the blues comes from wanting what you don't have. It takes time to train yourself to want less, to let go of desires, to act positively on dreams. Sometimes you are tired of waiting for these inner changes to take hold. When depression comes in any form, mild or severe, it slows or stops your progress. There is no easy answer, and we know it's part of personal growth to learn how to deal with these feelings. Every person on this planet experiences these feelings from time to time. Finding the path to happiness is learning how to deal with these feelings.

You can give in to the blues, eat that pint of Häagen-Dazs, watch four hours of mind-numbing television reruns, fix comfort food for dinner, or just sleep it off.

But there's an alternative: You can distract yourself by completely shifting gears. You can muster up the energy to do something challenging, like try a new recipe for dinner, clean the house, run a few miles. You have to let go of judgment if you take this route, because if you are down on yourself and the recipe does not work out perfectly, you don't want to end up feeling worse. So, it is important to let go of doubt and judgment and just let the results be.

As you know, this too will pass. Tomorrow or the next day will be better or different. You can learn from having the blues. Think of it as a growth opportunity. You can learn to be kind to yourself and give yourself a break. This can be a difficult thing for people to do, especially when they feel blue. Try to speak and act in a positive manner. Walk the positive path. Demonstrate to yourself how to let go and not get caught up in angry thoughts, passionate thoughts, worried thoughts, or depressed thoughts. Practice mindfulness, mindful breathing, and smiling. Your actions may be inspirational to family and friends who are also experiencing the blues.

66. Wear Comfort Clothes

Many of us dress nicely and wear full makeup even on the weekends, when we're just hanging out with our families and friends. We take pride in ourselves. In today's society, the type and style of clothes you wear seem to have a great deal of importance, and it's easy to get caught up in the fashion frenzy. We do the best we can.

But even your family will tell you that you are awfully cute when you put on those feety pajamas, the worn overalls, the schlumpy sweater and threadbare jeans, the funny furry slippers, the giant chenille robe. Sometimes there is nothing more therapeutic than comfort clothes. They just make us feel better. And, because you feel better, you look better. Your looks are coming from the inside out, and it shows.

These are the things you would wear all the time if no one was looking. Sometimes you are your best self when wearing comfort clothes. You are relaxed and restored. You are the person, not the clothes. But the question is: Can't you try to make your everyday clothes more like this? Can you experience the same feeling you have when you wear comfort clothes by wearing certain fabrics that are the same as your beloved comfort clothes?

Look carefully at your wardrobe and see if there are certain fabrics that are your favorites. I love soft wool and thick micro-chenille in the winter and pima cotton T-shirts in the summer. Uggs in the winter and flip-flops in the summer. I stay far, far away from "Dry Clean Only" and "Lay Flat to Dry."

In future purchases, add more clothing for your everyday wear that is quality comfort clothing. Along the way, you will develop a style all your own.

67. Be Aware of the Importance of Smell/Aroma

We each have our own scent that is as distinctive as our DNA, made from our hormones, hygiene, diet, and health. Your home has a distinctive scent, too, gathered up from pets, cleaning products and soaps, laundry, the pantry, flowers and plants, books, cooking, fireplace logs, etc. You can delight in your special aromas. These smells occupy a special place in your memory.

You can pay attention to the smells around you: the food court at the mall, the flowers at your table in the restaurant, rain changing the neighborhood fragrance. When you cook, you enjoy the intermingling of the ingredients. Coffee in the morning is an aphrodisiac for many. Then there's your perfume, scented powders and cosmetics, deodorant, toothpaste, and mouthwash. What about the smell of your kids' hair or your spouse's hand cream? There are so many personal smells that stir the memory, color emotions, and transform feelings and moods. You can use all of these to enhance your happiness. It does not matter who you are or what type of situation you are in, when you smell a pleasant aroma, it will have a positive impact on you.

Smell the aroma of freshly washed or brand-new clothes. Pay attention to the aroma, color, and feel of a flower. Select something with a smell you want to enjoy. Hold it near your nose. Be aware of changes in the experience of the smell as you become saturated with the odor. Be alert to sensations in your body as you breathe the smell in and out. Concentrate on the artistry of how the smell was created. Try to understand the precise chemical composition of the smell/aroma. After several minutes, move the item away. After several more minutes, move the item farther away. Stay alert to the possibility of smell and continue to be aware of breathing. Be mindful. Wake up to smell! Give thanks today for the gift of smell and make sure you inhale something wonderful.

68. See Like an Artist

Like many of you, I now need reading glasses. Because of the type of person I am, I have reading glasses in every room so I can quickly adjust my eyesight to see clearly. I need to be able to read and see the details, so I have gotten used to the routine and it works for me. However, reading glasses are not the only thing you need to see clearly. You need time to train yourself to see like an artist. True artists view the world, and life, differently than most people. Cultivating this can be fun and beneficial to your well-being.

The ability to see is a gift, and we often take it for granted. Every day, we need to be grateful for our sight and take care of it by really *seeing*. That's what this gift is for. Your eyes should be in love with the splendors of the world around you. Draw delight in seeing and wonder at the great gift of being able to see.

Merely looking at the world is immensely different from *seeing* it. Cats and dogs can look, but only humans have the capacity to see. Many of us, under the daily bombardment of photographic and electronic imagery, have lost that gift of seeing. But it can be learned anew so that we can once again see the world around us, as if for the first time.

This seeing consists of allowing the eye to be fully awake to life as it presents itself, uninterruptedly, in its myriad manifestations: the subtle variations in the apples on your table, a bird gathering sprigs of grass to build its nest, a woman pushing her baby carriage on a sidewalk at dusk. Even seeing things at different and multiple angles can have an impact on you. The more you look at life in order to really see things, the more happiness you create.

69. Savor

Many times when you try to recall what you ate or wore on the previous day, you find that you just can't remember. Why does this happen? We are so busy with what we consider to be "the big things," that we do not observe or perceive the smaller pleasures or miniature worlds within. What if, instead of just pulling on a pair of jeans, we took note of the orange thread used to sew them? What if we took that a step further and found out why this is true for most brands of jeans? This happened to me not too long ago. As I was grabbing a pair of jeans out of my closet, I just stopped and looked at them. I thought about blue jeans and what they've meant to me in my life. I remembered when we were first allowed to wear jeans to school. I was savoring my jeans. I looked more closely at their physical construction and wondered why they are sewn with orange thread. After I got dressed, I researched my question and found out that orange thread is used so it matches the copper rivets that double the durability of the jeans. I was savoring a small moment in my life and loving it.

Do you linger over coffee or tea in the morning, enjoying the aroma even before your first sip, and then feeling the hot liquid warming you from within? Or do you mindlessly sip your coffee and eat your breakfast while busily attending to some other task? When you complete a major task at work or home, do you take several moments to bask in the feeling of accomplishment, or are you more likely to move on to the next item on your to-do list? At the end of a long day, do you enjoy how good it feels to change into comfortable nightclothes and snuggle under the covers? Or are you more likely to spend your final waking moments considering problems of the day and planning for the next?

Noticing and savoring life's small (and big) pleasures is a powerful tool for increasing your overall happiness. Every day for the next week, be sure to savor at least two experiences (for example, your morning coffee, the sun on your face as you walk to your car, the sound of your child's voice). Totally immerse yourself in the moment and try not to think, just sense. Spend at least two to three minutes savoring each experience. Understand the impact that this savoring is having on your life. Become aware of this new feeling and enjoy it.

70. Practice Feng Shui

Feng shui (fung schway)? You have probably heard of this term, but maybe you're not sure about its exact meaning, or how it is used. Feng shui is a 4,000-year-old practice developed by the ancient Chinese to guide people toward the attainment of good health, wealth, and power. Today, feng shui principles are used by practitioners to help people live in harmony with nature rather than against nature. By applying some feng shui principles to your home, you'll optimize the flow of energy and minimize stagnation.

- *Use feng shui items such as mirrors and crystals for harmonious flow of chi (life energy).*
- *Separate pieces of furniture by three feet. Leaving space between pieces of furniture allows a continuous flow of energy.*
- *Hang brass wind chimes inside the front door for clarity.*
- *Put beds in front of a wall so you have a strong support behind you and elevate them so energy can flow freely underneath.*
- *Blue, green, or turquoise candles enhance knowledge, scholarly success, wisdom, experience, and self-development.*

- *Arrange furniture so that your back never faces a door. You should see your bedroom door from your bed. Your office door should be directly visible from your desk.*
- *Have books in plain view as you enter your home to increase insight.*
- *Limit the use of accessories, as they crowd space and reduce the flow of energy.*
- *Place pictures or paintings at eye level over a heavier piece of furniture.*
- *Use green to soothe the energy of your home.*
- *Eliminate clutter from your home. Place magazines in covered containers. File paperwork in filing cabinets. Use twist ties and surge protectors to consolidate cords and cables.*
- *Put mirrors at the end of hallways to minimize the feeling of a "dead end."*
- *Burn a yellow candle to promote calm and intelligence.*
- *Hang a round mirror in your bedroom to bring more love, compassion, and understanding to an intimate relationship.*
- *Place flowers in the bedroom, kitchen, and study to cultivate good luck.*
- *Hang a mirror adjacent to or behind your stove to reflect the burners, symbols of wealth and prosperity.*
- *Open your windows for at least twenty minutes daily to allow energy to flow from the outside into your home.*
- *Move twenty-seven objects that have not been moved in the last year to move forward out of a life rut.*

71. Tolerate Nothingness

What is nothingness? The understanding of "nothing" varies widely between cultures, especially between Western and Eastern cultures and philosophical traditions. Emptiness, different from "nothingness," is considered a state of mind in some forms of Buddhism. Achieving "nothing" as a state of mind allows people to be totally focused on a thought or activity at a level of intensity they would not be able to achieve if they were consciously thinking. The classic example of this is an archer drawing a bow, attempting to erase the mind as a way to better focus on the shot. The archer becomes the arrow.

When an artist begins a drawing or painting, he or she considers both positive shapes and negative spaces. The negative spaces surround the positive shapes and define them. What looks empty to the untrained eye appears to the artist's eye as a full, important entity. It is full of "nothing."

Though this concept may be confusing and somewhat difficult to understand, it is a concept worth trying to grasp. The key element you want to understand is that empty space is full of possibility, shrouded in the unknown until it is revealed. Do not try to fill every empty space. When you get rid of things, don't go looking for things to fill the space. Emptiness can have a positive influence. Think of the positive influence of emptying your mind during meditation!

Learn to tolerate more empty places; become more comfortable with waiting to fill what is empty with something truly worthwhile, or just accept the wonderful fullness of nothing. Nothingness can be very interesting.

72. Find and Acknowledge Your Passion

True happiness comes when you "do" what you're most passionate about. When you witness someone doing something with passion, the happiness within them is easy to see. It is time to find or acknowledge your own passion. The clues are all around you. Are you ignoring them? Have you kept your dreams a secret—even from yourself? Have you "buried" your innermost desires? Uncover your true passion and find real happiness.

Passion is a rich, soulful emotion. Whether it makes you feel angry, excited, inspired, or tearful, passion is something that moves you in a very powerful way. Passion is an internal experience, not an external event. Finding your passion means connecting your head with your heart, engaging that part of yourself that "feels" in a big, bold, spiritual way. For many of us, this is a challenge. Our busy, chaotic lives disconnect us from our feelings. And, when we act from this "numbed-out" place, it's impossible to connect with our passions. It is very easy to let this happen. To break this cycle takes effort.

If you already know what your passion is, you must get started. There's no time to waste! And if you have yet to identify your passion, here's a list of questions to get you started:

- *List five things that you want. List five things that you're good at. Do you know the difference between them?*
- *What interest, passion, or desire are you most afraid of admitting to yourself and others?*
- *What would you do if you knew you could not fail?*
- *What would you do if money was not a concern in your life?*

- *Who do you know who's doing something you'd like to do?*
- *What's stopping you from moving forward with exploring your passion?*
- *What drives you, and what gives you satisfaction?*
- *What would you regret not having done if your life was ending?*

73. Cook with Someone

Over the years, I have observed that most of the parties I attend or have at my place have something in common: They usually all end up in the kitchen. There must be something about the kitchen that brings joy and happiness to people. I believe it is our appreciation of food and the warmth of the kitchen that draw people there. One of the delights you can take part in, especially when children have left the nest, is cooking with your partner.

You can start by taking some cooking classes together, and then partner up in your own kitchen. If you have been the cook up to this point, you will have to learn to be gracious as you explain which pans and utensils are used for each task, and as you share your knowledge of cookbooks and how to follow cooking instructions. Sharing the kitchen with someone can be challenging, but you have to view this as part of the journey, and enjoy it. Hopefully, in this case, the end product will be almost as enjoyable as the journey!

You can each have an apron, a special towel—things like that to make the cooking process more ceremonial. Try not to put any time constraints on the cooking. Let it flow and enjoy where it takes you. Even if mistakes are made, do not fret over them. Do your best to fix them and move on. Even the best chefs in the world make errors.

And if your partner is not interested in this activity, look for a friend to share cooking with from time to time. It can be any meal, not just dinner. Whether a family member or a friend, cooking with someone can fill you up with much happiness. It's like choreography, working with someone else in the kitchen. Cooking can be a pleasurable and creative joint undertaking, every bit as enjoyable as the dining experience itself.

If you are feeling adventurous during a dinner party, put your guests to work sautéing, whisking, and chopping while you all chat. Then watch the fun and friendships grow. It will be remembered fondly by everyone involved.

74. Compile a List of Reminders

Part of the reason that quotations and poetry books are popular is that they offer "reminders" to us for finding more peace, love, and happiness. Something someone else says or writes can have a major impact on your life. There are some quotes I have read that have changed my entire outlook on life. A few sentences hit home, and everything changes. There's lots of advice, encouragement, and wisdom out there; you can gather your own collection of what's most meaningful to you and then post it where you will see these suggestions on a regular basis.

Some of my favorite quotations come from Henry David Thoreau, Ralph Waldo Emerson, and the Buddha. The wisdom I've acquired from their writings has added an important element to my life.

You'll have your own special ones, too. Whether you have a file where you keep quotations from magazines, page-a-day calendars, etc., or you write the quotations or poems into a notebook, they will serve you on many different levels. There are many resources out there; here is a beginning list of about ten to which you can add:

- *The grand essentials to happiness in this life are something to do, something to love, and something to hope for. (Joseph Addison)*
- *Perfect happiness is the absence of striving for happiness. (Chuang-Tse)*
- *There are as many nights as days, and the one is just as long as the other in the year's course. Even a happy life cannot be without a measure of darkness, and the word "happiness" would lose its meaning if it were not balanced by sadness. It is far better to take things as they come along with patience and equanimity. (Carl Jung)*
- *Very little is needed to make a happy life. It is all within yourself. (Marcus Aurelius)*
- *Slow down and enjoy life. It's not only the scenery you miss by going too fast—you also miss the sense of where you're going and why. (Eddie Cantor)*
- *We spend January 1 walking through our lives, room by room, drawing up a list of work to be done, cracks to be patched. Maybe this year, to balance the list, we ought to walk through the rooms of our lives ... not looking for flaws, but for potential. (Ellen Goodman)*

- *Craving only causes frustration; intense desire makes the object recede. If the game is really important, you're going to lose. If you're wildly in love, you're going to lose and you know it. The trick is to keep it from being that important. Be cool. Don't want it that much. Want it less. When you get to where you don't want it at all, then you're more likely to get it. And if you don't get it, you don't care so much. (Garrison Keillor)*
- *Show others, like your parents, how your choices make you happy. Make choices that reveal a deep sense of ease and happiness in your life. If your parents love you (and almost all parents do, even if they don't always seem to), they'll see this and be more inclined to accept your choices. (Buddha in Your Backpack)*
- *There is no way to happiness; happiness is the way. (The Buddha)*
- *Without looking out your window you can know the way of heaven. (George Harrison)*
- *Our life is frittered away by detail ... Simplify, simplify. (Thoreau)*
- *Like water, we are truest to our nature in repose. (Cyril Connolly)*
- *The aim of life is to live, and to live means to be aware, joyously, drunkenly, serenely, divinely aware. (Henry Miller)*
- *The whole of life lies in the verb seeing. (Teilhard de Chardin)*

75. Pursue Contentment

Being happy in one's situation in life is a sign of contentment. Being satisfied with adequate food, clothing, and shelter factors into the concept of contentment. By not letting any one activity dominate your day, you will cultivate an inner equilibrium and contentment. Develop gratitude for what you have been given.

The way to inner peace and contentment is as close as a cool tile floor, a rub on the belly, or a long walk with someone we love. If one has a sense of contentment and simplicity, that's enough. Meditation is a great tool for establishing an attitude of contentment. To be "content" means we're aware of our content. You feel full—content—when you open up to yourself and dive in.

There are other meditative pursuits that might bring you contentment. Some are knitting, needlepoint and cross-stitching, watercolor and oil painting, cooking. Things like drinking wine, eating gourmet food, working, and shopping are not what we are talking about.

Remember, it's the doing and being, not the wanting and desiring. We tend to forget that happiness does not come as a result of getting something we do not have, but rather of recognizing and appreciating what we do have. What passion (or passions) do you have, which, if you allowed yourself to pursue them, would bring you great happiness and contentment?

76. Find Time for Solitude

It's a well-known fact that our society suffers from a loss of solitude, and, at the same time, hungers for it. Solitude is beneficial for renewal and healing. Both types of solitude, bodily solitude and mental solitude, should be cultivated. Sometimes it is easy to find time for solitude, but even when it is difficult, you still need to make an effort. You will benefit from it.

Bodily solitude means being physically alone. I don't mean to say that we should avoid being with people. Rather, I mean we should spend time by ourselves. As humans, needing bodily solitude is part of our makeup. People tend to enjoy bodily solitude for short periods of time, so loneliness does not set in. However, there is no set time limit for this practice. Each person is different and requires different amounts of alone time. We need to be alone in order to have a chance at gaining mental stillness. Remember, some bodily solitude is also important when practicing meditation.

Mental solitude means not thinking about anything in particular, but being alert and aware. Mental solitude lets us eliminate many of the things that prevent spiritual growth. Some people believe that when we are not thinking about anything, then we must be asleep or somehow dulled to our surroundings. Some people don't understand the importance of mental solitude; craving constant stimulation, they want to be with somebody who can provide a fun atmosphere. When there is nothing to stimulate them, they become bored. Even when they are alone bodily, they read or watch TV, listen to the radio or iPod, or think about things they've done or will do. They don't consider it a productive use of time to simply be alone, not reading or watching TV, not listening to the radio or iPod, and not thinking about things.

You should be encouraged to claim your own solitude and the gifts that are given in that quiet space. You can find your own personal place of solitude. Certain parts of ourselves are only tapped when we are alone. The artist, the writer, the musician, the spiritual seeker—all have to work alone. You, too, will benefit when you can experience solitude.

When finding time for solitude is difficult, there are some steps you can take to help you. Wake up a half-hour before everyone else, or take a few minutes after everyone leaves for work or school or after others go to bed. You can take your lunch hour alone. Taking a walk by yourself is also a good way to find solitude. Staying in bed for an entire weekend morning can do the trick. Even if you and your family members are apart during the day, it is still important to have some quality time alone at home, maybe a couple of nights a week. Use this time for your own personal renewal.

77. Get a Pet

Owning a pet can create happiness in our lives. Most of us have learned about unconditional love from a pet. They love us no matter how we feel, what we look like, how much money we have. They all have their quirks, but they offer constant companionship, pretty much without question. Scientists say that loving, caring for, and spending time with animals enhances our well-being. Some of the health benefits associated with owning a pet are lowering blood pressure and cholesterol levels, as well as decreasing feelings of loneliness. You may know or have an emotional bond with a pet.

You can talk to pets and they say nothing. They are the ultimate listeners (and they never tell your secrets). In a world filled with constant noise, this is something to cherish.

Think of a cat, asleep much of the time yet acutely aware of what is going on around it. The cat is simply being itself wholeheartedly.

It is in the present moment, open to whatever occurs. Cats are Zen masters sent to teach us about being rather than doing.

Be grateful for your creatures and their love. Open your heart to them and they will return the type of devotion that most of us can only dream about receiving from human beings.

78. Define Success Your Way

Success really should be a personal matter, defined by—and different for—each of us. My definition of success includes finding time to pursue my passion, having loving relationships, and developing my spiritual life. It is about examining and knowing who I am so that I can be the best possible representation of myself. Take some time to develop your own definition of success. Analyze how you are meeting your definition. If you are honest with yourself, this will be a growth opportunity for you.

When I think about success, I also think about death. When I die, will I have regrets? Will I feel that I have spent too much time on certain things and not enough on others? Thinking about death in this way, at any point in my life, is useful to me because I can do a course correction. I can understand myself better and hopefully correct my path if necessary.

Success also means acceptance and tolerance and kindness for yourself. If you are doing the best you can, what more can you do? You try to give back to the world, to serve in some way to show your gratitude for being alive. You try to make a difference in other people's lives through kindness. It is not about attainment, accomplishment, stuff, money. If you know your strengths and values and work with them, certain things will fall into place. You will have enough to pay the bills, and some to save and share.

True success is more about letting go, knowing that you have everything you need already. It is discovering that being is as important as doing. Yes, you will pursue goals, but you understand that things change; that we are all interconnected; and that you do not have control of your life. You do the best you can and let go. It's about being happy right now in the present moment.

79. Do What You Love

There are lots of sayings like "Do what you love, and the money will follow," and "To love what you do and feel that it matters—how could anything be more fun?" And those who are familiar with the Buddha's Noble Eightfold Path know that Right Livelihood is part of the scheme. While it's important to discover your Right Livelihood, it has to start with knowing yourself.

Having a sense of purpose and striving to achieve your goals give life meaning, direction, and satisfaction. It not only contributes to health and longevity, but also makes you feel better in difficult times. Do you look forward to going to work? Do you have a sense of purpose? Below are a set of questions to help you discover what you love.

- *Identify what's important to you. What does success mean to you? Don't try to live up to others' expectations and definitions of success. Learn how to say no politely.*
- *Consider how you'd change your life if you knew you had six months to live. If you would change jobs, return to school,*

complete a project, then maybe it's time to get on with it! What's stopping you?

- Concentrate on the present. Don't take your life for granted. What do you really want to accomplish? Who do you want to be?
- Figure out what you'd do if money didn't matter. If you're working at something that has no meaning just to pay the bills, you're making money more important than your sense of purpose. How could you make money doing what you enjoy?
- To identify your purpose, look for themes that emerge from the foregoing exercises as well as these questions: What are your strengths and accomplishments? What do you want your colleagues to say about your contributions? What would you do if you were a billionaire? What activities absorbed you as a young child?
- What kind of person do you want to be five years from now? Who do you admire? What skills, interests, and needs do you want to use in your ideal job?

Once you've answered these questions, you may need to research occupations that might fit your dream career. Specify a goal that will enable you to attain your occupational preference, and make plans to achieve that goal. Be flexible; your goals may change as you get to know yourself better. Purpose is a common denominator for success and failure. Knowing your purpose will give you the courage to do what you've always longed to do. You'll be empowered to achieve your goals. It will be easier to take risks, to manage your fears. You'll be able to change your life for the better.

80. Quiet Your Wants

Shopping is truly an addiction. People shop from greed, desire, craving, and wanting. They are trying to fill an emptiness in their soul. Trying to fill a Hungry Ghost—a Buddhist metaphor for people futilely attempting to fulfill their illusory physical desires. This addiction does not have a happy ending. Lives are filled with stuff and debt. It can become a vicious cycle. Your stress level can increase tremendously as your debt load increases. To achieve the perception of happiness, you buy more. Up goes the debt even further. The cycle continues until you realize what's happening and attempt to stop it. Another common trap people fall into with buying things is when they try to buy love through purchasing things for others. Even if you can afford it, you are sending the wrong message. It is not a healthy habit for your soul.

Ask yourself what it is you truly want. What do your temporary acquisitions fulfill for you? Is desire, greed, or discontent the cause? Ask yourself: Do I become consumed by the objects of my momentary desire? Do I have a Hungry Ghost?

Consider the cravings and compulsions in your life. What do you feel you cannot live without? What price are you willing to pay for it? What kind of fulfillment does this craving or compulsion provide? Look at the questions gently, without judging. Wait for responses to come. Allow change to occur; it will anyway.

Explore desire for a day or for a week. Notice your relationship to it. Meditate on it: see it arise, observe its features, soften and receive it, let it go. You can quiet your wants by acknowledging them rather than pushing them away and denying their presence.

The best exercise of all is to keep a list of what you think you want. Put it away and then check on it in a week or a month, but before checking it, try to recall what was on the list. A major clue that you don't really need or want anything on the list is if you can't remember anything on it! But even if you can remember what is on the list, see if you really still want the items when you check back.

81. *Flow*

Psychologist Mihály Csíkszentmihályi proposed the term *flow* for the mental state of operation in which the person is fully immersed in what he or she is doing, characterized by a feeling of energized focus, full involvement, and success in the process of the activity. You know what it is when you are working on a project and hours pass without your realizing it. Or you are playing basketball "in the zone." You are alert, exhilarated, joyful, entranced with your experience.

For millennia, practitioners of Buddhism and Taoism have honed the discipline of overcoming the duality of self and object as a central feature of spiritual development. Eastern spiritual practitioners have developed a very thorough and holistic set of theories around overcoming duality of self and object, tested and refined through spiritual practice instead of the systematic rigor and controls of modern science. The phrase *being at one with things* (overcoming the separateness of self and object) is a metaphor of Csíkszentmihályi's flow concept.

Reading Csíkszentmihályi's *Flow* is the best way to understand how to bring more into your life. Ritual plays a part, as does variety and challenge. But self-forgetfulness is at the heart of flow. You are not self-conscious, you forget yourself, and you are fully absorbed in the task. You are doing something challenging that requires competency and has a clear goal. You concentrate on it and simultaneously have a sense of control and effortless involvement. Time stops. Flow creates deep gratification. Those who experience flow consider themselves happier and more optimistic than others.

One way to get started is to write down three times when you experienced flow, when you felt the most alive. What were you doing? How could you do that more often? The more you challenge yourself mentally, physically, and spiritually, the greater the sense of gratification you will experience.

82. Handle the Holidays

Holiday celebrations should, in an ideal world, provide an opportunity to experience myriad cultures and traditions, allow you to connect with loved ones, reflect on the past, and become energized for the future. In real life, that can seem as likely as the rooftop landing of eight tiny reindeer.

Instead, the mad sprint from November to January involves overindulging at the office holiday party, fretting over the perfect Hanukkah gift, and spending way too much on stuff no one really needs. It's enough to make you want to disappear every December and not return until well into the new year. We get caught up in a very materialistic interpretation of the holiday season. How many times have you heard just after Halloween, "They have the Christmas decorations up already?!"

It doesn't have to be that way. Somewhere between avoidance and toxic levels of gluttony, there is a middle road. If you're mindful, you can appreciate the season instead of having to roll around it. A term that I like to utilize during the holidays is *nonattachment*. People confuse nonattachment with nonparticipation or indifference. The true meaning of *nonattachment* is a full-out, full-body embrace of life; it's being able to embrace the colors and sounds without getting sucked in.

If ever there is a time to stick to routines, this is it. Get plenty of sleep, eat well, and redouble your commitment to exercise. If you maintain balance most of the time, you can enjoy the season's indulgences and recover from them more quickly.

However you overhaul your holiday, the aim isn't just to concentrate on your own desires, but to be aware of the choices you have. Let go of the "shoulds" and see if you can figure out what truly makes you happy. One exercise is to list the elements of an ideal December, then dissect the most appealing ideas. If you want to host a dinner, ask yourself why. Is it because you love to cook? You want to get the family together? Or do you think it would make someone else happy? Once you know your motives, you can plan an event that makes everyone happy: Take time off so you can do the party and enjoy it; host a tea party rather than dinner; or drop the whole idea and invite someone to go to lunch instead.

83. Read

Reading anytime is a great refuge. Reading can take you anywhere in the world. It can let you feel all of the human emotions. You should never try to read something out of a sense of obligation. If you don't like a book after ten (or fifty) pages, there are millions of other books out there. Know your style of reading (maybe you like short chapters of fiction or nonfiction) and favorite genres. No matter what type of reader you are, you can definitely find books that will make you happy.

Reading inserts ideas and knowledge into your head. It gets and keeps the wheels spinning. There are lots of times when you read something that transports you, that makes you feel warm and fuzzy inside, that inspires you and gets your creative juices flowing— something more than a few words but less than a paragraph, that gives you ideas or lets you learn something or simply moves your soul. You can take notes from your reading, phrases and sentences and passages that you want to remember. You can create your own "commonplace book" of all that you capture from other authors.

Students compiled these commonplace books years ago in the course of their readings in order to create a stock of ideas for their own speeches and compositions. They were a way to compile knowledge, usually by writing information into books. They were essentially scrapbooks filled with items of every kind: medical recipes, quotes, letters, poems, tables of weights and measures, proverbs, prayers, legal formulas. Commonplace books were used by readers, writers, students, and humanists as an aid for remembering useful concepts or facts they had learned. Each commonplace book was unique to its creator's particular interests.

From a book called *Lost in a Book: The Psychology of Reading for Pleasure*:

> Reading for pleasure is an extraordinary activity. The black squiggles on the white page are as still as the grave, colorless as the moonlit desert; but they give the skilled reader a pleasure as acute as the touch of a loved body, as rousing, colorful and transfiguring as anything out there in the real world. And yet, the more stirring the book, the quieter the reader; pleasure reading breeds a concentration so effortless that the absorbed reader of fiction (transported by the book to some other place, and shielded by it from distractions), who is so often reviled as an escapist and denounced as the victim of a vice as pernicious as tippling in the morning, should instead be the envy of every student and every teacher.

84. Express Gratitude Directly

The expression of gratitude is most effective when done directly—in person, by phone, by letter. If there is someone in particular to whom you owe a debt of gratitude, try expressing your appreciation in concrete terms. Maybe it's your sister, favorite aunt, or an old friend; a coach, teacher, or supervisor from the past.

Write a letter now. Describe in detail what he or she did for you and exactly how it affected your life. Tell how often you remember his or her efforts. If possible, visit and read the letter out loud and in person. You could do this on an anniversary, birthday, holiday, or random day.

Some people find it uplifting to write gratitude letters to people whom they do not know personally but who have influenced their lives, such as authors and politicians. Others write letters to people who have made their lives easier, like a bank clerk, customer service representative, or librarian.

Tests run by scientists clearly show that people who write gratitude letters experience an increased sense of well-being. Those who presented the letters in person had the largest boosts in happiness, and the boosts lasted longer. Writing gratitude letters is something you can do on a regular basis. Even if you write a letter and choose not to send it, it is still a worthwhile activity.

85. Make a List of Goals

It is a good idea to identify your long-range goals and break them up into shorter-term or subgoals. In your journal writing, you may have written down goals for the next one, two, or even five years. You describe what you would like to have accomplished by then, and what you would like your life to be like.

To go further with this, you could then write about the steps you will take to reach that point. There may be many paths or steps, not just one. If you find pessimistic or doubtful thoughts entering your mind, note these and try to create alternative scenarios or possible resolutions. You can remember times in the past when you have been successful at something, recognizing the strengths and resources that you already have and allowing that to motivate you.

A few simple techniques can help you set realistic but challenging goals. First, you must state the goal positively. If you set a goal of never eating dessert again, you'll only find yourself obsessing about dessert. Instead, vow to eat more healthful desserts. Second, the goal should be specific. You have to know when you reach it. A lot of people, when they get close to their goal, always move the bar a little further, so they're never quite there. It's important to be able to say, "Hey, I did it." And then you can set a new goal. Third, the goal must be important to *you*—not to your friends, your boss, your husband, or your father.

Finally, the goal must be something you can control. A goal that aims to change another person's behavior violates this principle. So, too, does an ambition to land a specific new job. Any goal you set your sights on—whether it's being the first female vice president of your corporation, winning a marathon, or losing fifty pounds—involves many factors outside of your control. And even when a goal does depend mostly on your own actions, you can never perform perfectly at all times. So it's important to focus on your behaviors and get real about what you can and can't control.

86. Makeg Time for a Relationship

It is worth the effort to strengthen intimate or romantic relationships. Even if your relationship is already good and solid, there is always room to strengthen and enjoy it more.

The first secret of success is to talk—a lot. Commit to extra time each week with your partner, starting with one hour. Spend at least five minutes every day expressing appreciation or gratitude for things he or she does (behaviors). Before you leave on a workday, find out one thing that the other person is going to do that day. When you see each other again, you can bring it up and listen to your partner talk about it. Sometimes you have to get creative, but it can help a lot. Scheduling time for a date in the evening, a lunch together, a Sunday morning is very important. You can go on a hike together, take a drive, cook together, or go to dinner and a movie.

Even more important, you need to express admiration, affection, and appreciation for each other. Make it a goal to raise the number of positive things you do in this area. Do this directly.

Take delight in your partner's good fortune. Resolve to respond actively and constructively, with interest and enthusiasm, to your loved one's good news, however small. And, in whatever ways you can, help develop a deep sense of shared rituals, dreams, and goals to help your relationship thrive. Sharing an inner or spiritual life is a way of honoring and respecting each other. If both people in the relationship attempt to make more time for each other, and enjoy and respect this time, happiness will follow this union.

87. Stop Overthinking and Ruminating

It can be very compelling to overthink our problems; it's a natural tendency for everyone. You believe that if you think about something enough, you will be able to figure things out. However, at some point you can cross a line where it becomes overthinking and ruminations. Overthinking causes stress and insecurity to escalate. No insight is gained from overthinking. Rumination only makes things worse. There are three steps to stop this behavior if you persistently fall into the trap.

First, free yourself as soon as you recognize you are overthinking. Distract yourself with an activity engrossing enough that you can't lapse back into ruminations. That usually means doing something that makes you feel amused, curious, happy, or peaceful. The positive emotions received from distracting yourself will be useful in the future, too. A lift in mood can energize you. There are other possible strategies, like telling yourself "No!" or "Stop!" Or you can set an amount of time aside each day to do the thinking and then let it go. Another strategy is to use a journal to pour out the thoughts and ruminations and then let them go by shutting the journal. Whatever approach you take, the important thing is to recognize that you are overthinking.

Second, you need to gain a new perspective on yourself and on your life in general. This means acting immediately, taking whatever steps you can to address problems that you can solve or start to resolve. There is no time to procrastinate here. Many situations can be resolved quickly by taking whatever steps you can to correct them. For example, let's say you made unflattering remarks about someone and it got back to them. Take immediate action and apologize without delay. Tell the person that you learned a valuable lesson and you are sorry that you hurt him or her. You have eliminated time that you could have spent overthinking the situation. Sometimes it takes longer than we would like to resolve something, but at least you are trying to do something about it. The longer you wait before you begin a plan of action, the more stress develops and the unhealthier it becomes.

Finally, you need to learn how to avoid future overthinking traps. If certain people, places, situations, or seasons trigger your overthinking—then you can avoid them or modify them enough to thwart their abilities as triggers. This is similar to what a smoker has to do to quit, or what an overeater has to do to slow food intake. Learning to meditate can be one of the best things you can do to help yourself recognize and deal with overthinking and ruminations. Regular meditation helps you feel less burdened, stressed, and worried. It helps you let go of anger and forgive more easily, too.

88. Hug

Frequent hugging is endorsed by many as a way to increase happiness. It is an intimacy and friendship booster. A hug can relieve stress, make you feel closer to someone, and even diminish pain.

For people you love, when approaching, put your hands on their shoulders and look them in the eyes. Say you love them, how much you care for them, and how much you are loving every second with them. Be welcoming when you hug. If you or someone asks for a hug, then be warm and loving, and just make it feel like the person you're hugging is safe; make him or her feel like the two of you are the only people that matter at that moment. When you truly hug a loved one, the world becomes very small. It feels like you two are the only ones in the universe. It creates a special feeling.

Do not leave anybody out who might want to be hugged. Learn to hug for the person. Different people need different types of hugs. Your adult children may need to feel special; hug them like you did when they were children. A close friend may need to know that you support her; hug her to give her your strength. When you hug Grandma, don't squeeze too hard (you don't want to hurt her). In most cases, hugs are appropriate, so try not to downplay the importance of a hug. The person giving the hug may feel that he or she needs to give you one.

If you're angry at a loved one, hug that person—and mean it. You may not want to, which is all the more reason to do so. It's hard to stay angry when someone shows he or she loves you, and that's precisely what happens when we hug each other.

89. Cope by Writing

Writing about something upsetting or even traumatic can positively affect your health and well-being. It is a great coping tool to use in times of trouble and confusion. You should write about the experience in detail and fully explore your personal reactions and deepest emotions. Since this is only for you, you need to be completely honest with yourself. You should write for fifteen to thirty minutes, and continue doing this for three to five days.

Such expressive writing about upsetting or traumatic events has many beneficial results, such as enhanced immune function and less depression and distress. The nature of the writing process helps us understand, come to terms with, and make sense of upset and trauma. Finding meaning in the pain through writing also seems to reduce how often and intensely a person experiences intrusive thoughts about the event.

Writing about the experience in a journal forces you to organize and integrate your thoughts and images into a coherent narrative. Language, because it is highly structured, triggers an analysis that could help you find meaning, enhanced understanding, and a sense of control. This is a by-product of the writing process. When an experience has structure and meaning, it seems more manageable to you.

The process of creating a narrative about your experience can lead you to accept it. Writing involves recording your thoughts externally, whether on paper or in the computer. This may allow you to unburden yourself by chronicling your emotions, memories, and thoughts, ultimately allowing you to move past your troubles. Your coping abilities will naturally be strengthened by this process.

90. Write a Letter of Forgiveness

Writing a letter of forgiveness is an exercise that involves letting go of your anger, bitterness, and blame by writing—but not sending—a letter of forgiveness to a person who has hurt or wronged you. It's not the actual sending of the letter that is important here, but the practice of forgiveness. In life, we sometimes feel that we have been wronged by people. Whether these infractions are big or small, they are real to us and have a negative impact on our lives. Many times, the person who hurt us is not even aware that he or she did something unkind.

What experiences remain in your memory, unforgiven, that you dwell on, staying hurt or offended or angry? Do any of these experiences keep you from feeling happy? If so, forgiveness is vital. Forgiveness sets you free. The forgiveness letter talks about what happened, what you wish the other person had done instead, and then ends with an explicit statement of forgiveness and understanding. You are unburdened by the process and now can move forward.

This may be hard to do if you view the act as unforgivable and you feel too overwhelmed by negative feelings to start letting it go. If that is true, just try. You might have to set the letter aside and come back to it at a later time. Forgiveness takes effort, motivation, and willpower. Forgiveness must be practiced in order for you to live a happy life.

91. Train Your Attention

It is very important to develop a state of mind called *immovable wisdom*. It means having fluidity around an unmoving center, so that your mind is clear and ready to direct its attention wherever it may be needed. The mind never stops. You need to have your mind move freely, spontaneously, and flexibly. No matter what circumstance lies in front of you, you will be mindful of your situation. Mindfulness is clear comprehension, paying attention to what you are doing, knowing whether actions are skillful or unskillful. The moment one gives close attention to anything, even a blade of grass, it becomes a mysterious, awesome, indescribably magnificent world unto itself.

Anyone can become more fully engaged and involved in the experiences of daily life, cultivating flow. The secret is attention. What you notice and pay attention to is your experience. Attention needs to be directed fully to the task at hand. When you are concentrating on doing something, you are directing your attention to that task.

In the midst of speaking, working, cleaning, or any other activity, stop for a moment. Be aware of where you are and be aware of your breathing. Actively take your attention from the external world and focus it on your breath. This is a way to train your attention. You will be surprised at how much more engaged and involved in life you become after doing this.

At the beginning of each week, choose a simple regular activity that you usually do on autopilot. Resolve to make that particular activity into a reminder to wake up your mindfulness. You could choose making tea or coffee, shaving, bathing, watering the plants, turning on lights, etc. Resolve to pause for a few seconds each time before you start the activity. You then carry it out with gentle and complete attention. Try to bring mindfulness to this act each time. Each week, add another activity until you have four areas of daily mindfulness.

92. Keep Learning

Whether I am working or doing pleasurable activities, I have one rule in my life: I have to be learning. I plan on learning until the day I die. I am proud of this philosophy. I feel that I have learned many great things and have many more fantastic things to learn. I have studied archaeology, art, Buddhist studies, cooking, list making, organizing, and many more topics. I have read dictionaries and encyclopedias. All of this is part of my everyday life. I have found happiness in life because I choose to live this way.

Learning new things every day is what makes children happy, so why not adults? Maybe it's what you learn in a crossword puzzle, a word from your page-a-day calendar, a fun fact or how something works from the Internet, or a new philosophy from reading a book. This comes pretty easily for children, but a little more work is required for adults. Remember that an old dog *can* learn new tricks!

This is not really that hard. We all know how tedious life is when nothing is new and nothing is challenging. You can change that yourself by adding learning on a daily basis. Read four pages of a dictionary or encyclopedia. Read a chapter on how things work in your home. Read a chapter of a cookbook. Yes, nonfiction!! It expands many people's horizons.

But it is not just about reading. Do not limit your learning to reading only. Learning can come in the form of painting, drawing, or doodling; trying knitting or needlepoint, pottery or weaving; or perfecting your tennis serve. There are no parameters to follow. The learning you choose to do should be pretty darned selfish, learning about things you really want to know more about. Gaining knowledge in any way you choose will add more meaning and happiness to your life.

93. Find a New Approach to the Routine

There's plenty of routine in everyday life, and we have talked about how being mindful and meditative can change tedious experiences into something more meaningful and stimulating. Another approach is to attempt shorter, more intense activities—called *microflow*—with specific goals and rules. Examples are solving math problems in your head, like figuring out the tip at a restaurant;

drawing a comic strip; creating funny lyrics to a song you hear all the time. While you wait in the dentist's waiting room, instead of reading *Skiing* magazine, why not make a birthday wish list or try to draw something you see in the room?

The next time you are brushing your teeth, find a challenging and interesting little activity to do in your head. Invent a private activity that provides just enough challenge for you to not be completely bored, but is also so automated that it leaves enough attention free so that if something interesting happens, it will register in your awareness. During a boring work meeting, you may doodle intricate designs in the margins of your notebook. This type of activity provides sufficient challenge but does not distract you to the point where you cannot pay attention to the person conducting the meeting.

Microflow activities help people overcome boring, tedious situations in which escape is usually impossible without consequences (like business meetings). Enjoyment appears at the boundary of boredom and anxiety, when the challenges are balanced with the person's capacity to act.

94. Take Pleasure in Each Sense

Use your heart, soul, and senses to live. The more you let your senses open up, the better. The brain rewires itself daily to be better at what we are paying attention to. When you exercise a sense, the brain makes more neural connections for that sensory pathway. When you connect that sense with other senses, the brain makes connective pathways to coordinate perceptions. This is one of the things that makes meditation fun: You progressively have richer experiences of your world as you move through daily life. It is in your control to achieve this.

Meditate on happiness. Just let whatever thoughts and images come to your mind be there. When they trail off, turn your senses within and meditate on what your real happiness is. You will know when you find it, because you will feel a deep, ecstatic inner glow. Slowly relax and return to normal. The inner glow of happiness will continue with you for some time. Take a moment and attune yourself to it.

Tell yourself that you would like to remember certain life experiences, those particular times when your senses were deeply involved in an activity. You may call them *peak experiences*. As your mind sifts and categorizes these, one in particular will assert itself strongly. Focus on it. Let yourself go and relive this timeless moment of *presentness*. Do not try to change it. Open to it with calm awareness.

Luxuriating or indulging in the senses is one way to promote savoring. Pay close attention to momentary pleasures and wonders: the sweetness of a ripe peach, the smells from a bakery, the warmth of the sun when you step outside. Roll in the moment, fully absorbing the experience.

95. Follow Your Spirituality

Be a spiritual adventurer; be audacious. Take risks; search everywhere. Do not let a single opportunity or chance that life offers pass you by. Take breaks throughout the day to recharge your spiritual batteries. Appreciate that you are a spiritual being having a physical experience, rather than a physical being having a spiritual experience.

Whether you are creating your spiritual life from scratch or adding to an existing one, think about the spare parts and tools you already possess. Become aware of everything that is already available to you. Are there prayers that you already know by heart? How about hymns and songs? Meditations? All are useful in your quest.

Passages can be read for inspiration on your own personal journey, or can even be memorized for use in *passage meditation*, a path of spiritual growth and discipline practiced for many centuries. In this mode of meditation, one trusts the inspired passage to be the seed of the spiritual experience attained by its author. By memorizing and continually repeating its words silently in the mind, you gradually absorb this experience. Eventually, passage meditation slows and even stills your mind, and then you perceive what lies in the space between your thoughts. When your mind becomes thus stilled, abiding in this interstice between thoughts, a sudden flash can illuminate your nature and show you who you really are and have always been.

Finally, think of your difficult times as spiritual training. A life cannot be lived without difficult times. Embrace your difficulties and appreciate them for providing new ways to grow spiritually. Try to think of the positive benefits and spiritual lessons that troubles can almost certainly provide. Enjoy the process. Don't add suffering. Accepting and embracing difficulties softens you and makes you more tolerant of change. See more of the big picture through spiritual study and contemplation in order to gain greater knowledge and power in how you create karma.

96. Act Like a Happy Person

Have people told you that you could win an Oscar for your acting talent? We all have the ability to "act," so why not act like a happy person? Pretending that you are happy can not only earn you some of the benefits of happiness (smiles, friendship, success), but can actually make you happier. If you smile, the world smiles with you. I am not talking about fakery. I do not want you to act happy for a second when you meet people and then as soon as they are out of earshot you turn sad or angry. I want the act to last for a long time. Do not turn it on and off. Leave it on for a while.

If you act like a happy person, people respond to you more positively. Smiling and laughter can help dislodge negative emotions, distract you from worries or ruminations, and bring amusement, joy, and peace. Any type of smile or laughter gives you, at the very least, a mild feeling of positive well-being. It boosts you toward being able to cope better and be more tolerant, reducing anxiety and stress while bringing happiness.

Think of someone you know who is genuinely happy. How does that person walk through a room? How does he or she talk about things? Try zipping yourself into that person's "personality suit." Really focus on embracing that person's approach to life for an hour or two. Chances are it will feel better than the suit you've been wearing. Act as if you are optimistic and happy and see what happens. It could lead to an award that you give yourself for filling your life with more happiness.

97. Add Variety to Your Life

"Variety is the spice of life" is one of my favorite sayings. Isn't life much better when it's filled with a variety of the things we like? Of course it is. It is inevitable that some things in your life will go wrong, so it's nice to have other things that you still enjoy to fall back on. As with investing, "Don't put all of your eggs in one basket." The same goes for our personal lives. The way to be happy is to fill our lives with a range of things that make us happy. This decreases the risk of becoming unhappy if some of the things go wrong. Don't risk your happiness by failing to broaden your horizons. One way to add diversity to your life is to explore several different hobbies. If you have an idea of something you would like to do, then go and do it.

What makes people decide to not fill their lives with a variety of activities that make them happy? There are a thousand excuses. Sometimes it is money or time. But if you just prioritize your money and time better, you should be able to pursue any interest or hobby you have. Other times you feel tired or have a parental responsibility. I am not trying to get you to give up your parental responsibilities, but instead, I'm encouraging you to find a solution so you have time for both. Adding variety to your life will create a more balanced life for yourself and give you more energy to do more things. In fact, by pursuing personal interests outside of work, you can increase your effectiveness in the workplace. Everyone needs a recreational break from working all the time. Try not to let an excuse or guilt get in your way of pursuing a variety of activities that fill your life with spice.

Now that you are excited about spicing up your life and have eliminated all the excuses and guilt, take a few minutes to look at the following steps to help you out.

- *Sit down and think of anything you would like to pursue.*
- *Write down how you can do it and what it will take.*
- *Go after it.*

I have found that spending just a half-hour a day doing something I enjoy can really make a difference. It might take a little time to develop some new hobbies, but it will be worth it in the end.

98. Be Kind

Everyone wants to be happy. How can we do it in such a way that increases joy and lessens suffering in ourselves and others? How can we treat ourselves and others compassionately in trying to achieve happiness? The Dalai Lama says, "If you want others to be happy, practice compassion. If you want to be happy, practice compassion."

This means being as kind as possible to yourself and those around you. There is an inextricable relationship between happiness and kindness. Just be kind, right now. No matter the circumstances, be kind. Whether it is a family member, friend, lover, someone on the street, someone who seems to hate you, or little old you. Just be kind in whatever way is appropriate.

Try to remember a time when someone was kind to you, a small act of kindness, or a large one. Focus on the details. Remember how appreciative you were. Remember how good you felt and how many times you told the story surrounding the event. The feeling is pretty powerful, and, the best part, it's available to you through recall.

Practicing compassion and kindness to ourselves and others gives us happiness. The more you treat others well, the happier you will feel. Kindness is the starting point, the fount from which flows so many other positive qualities, such as forgiveness, generosity, honesty, and patience.

Kindness creates a sense of warmth and openness that allows us to communicate more easily with others. This generates a spirit of friendship. Fostering the trait of kindness not only leads to our individual happiness and the happiness of those around us, but will also guide us in a world that has become somewhat anxious, cold, difficult, and frightening. For our life to be of value, we need to nurture compassion and kindness.

99. Wait for the End of the Story

It's been a while since you've talked to your son, who's in college. The last time you talked to him, he had gotten into trouble and didn't fully know the consequences he'd face for the incident. Now it has been several days. You are creating all kinds of scenarios in your head.

You made a pretty big mistake at work. You owned up to it and developed a plan of action to correct the error. You also admitted to learning a valuable lesson. But you are still worried about keeping your job. Shouldn't you wait for the end of the story before freaking out?

These types of things happen to us all the time.

You can make a choice here: You can refuse to get all worked up about something until you get to the end of the story. How many people have worried that someone got in an accident just because he or she was late coming home? How many people have worried that their spouse is having an affair just because they stayed late at work one night? If you find yourself worrying, try reminding yourself that you don't know the end of the story yet. It has to play out. Then, you can start worrying about it, or, rather, work on fixing it (if that is required, or can be done). Just think about how much time and energy you waste when you speculate as to what *may* happen. Wait for the end of the story and use that time and energy in productive ways.

Waiting for the end of the story keeps you from creating a list of all the things that could go wrong, things that most likely will never come to pass. Waiting for the end of the story allows you to put what is happening now into some type of perspective so you can be happier in the present moment, no matter what is going on.

Unless you are a psychic, your guesses about how things will end in any given situation are probably wrong, anyway! If you wait for the end of the story, you can live a more graceful and happier life. You can appreciate the present moment. Everything is impermanent and everything changes. Even if the end of the story produces the worst-case scenario, by waiting and putting everything into perspective, you will be able to deal with it more effectively. This too shall pass.

100. Be Optimistic

One method that will give you some power in creating happiness is to take the optimistic view, to look at what is right in any given moment or situation, to look at the bright side of life. Focusing on what is right is an agent for powerful change. Training yourself in the art of positive thinking does take practice. But the increased level of happiness in your life makes it worth it.

The more you recognize your potentials, strengths, and successes, the happier you will feel. It's like turning your face toward the sun. In life, we all have to examine problems and deal with unpleasant situations, but by focusing on the positive, we are better able to come up with solutions.

Research has established that some people are born with optimistic traits. Optimism comes very naturally to them. It may not come naturally to you. The good news is, you can learn to think more optimistically. It is really important to enjoy life. It doesn't make any sense to refuse to appreciate the gift of life. Looking at the bright side, called *learned optimism*, means training yourself to change your explanatory style—the way you explain the good and bad things that happen to you. Switching from pessimism to learned optimism is a decision *you* make.

You may not be able to control what happens to you, but you do have some control over your emotions. When adversity strikes, how you think and what you believe will determine how you feel and what you do. Optimism in difficult situations helps people to grow. Learned optimism is founded on the principle of seeing life situations accurately, hence reducing catastrophic explanations for everyday circumstances.

101. Love

What is your definition of love? Is there more than one kind of love? Here are a few questions to ponder while you look at this section. It can't hurt to expand your idea of love. Love is clearly part of happiness. It is probably the most powerful emotion we feel. True happiness is unselfish love that increases in proportion as it is shared. To allow love to become an important part of happiness, we have to think of love beyond romantic terms, and even beyond family connections. You can look at love in a spiritual way, too.

A happy life, for most, also includes genuine friendships, lasting bonds to others. It means opening our hearts to care for and about others. If we restricted our definition of love, then we would be missing out on lots of ways we could find joy in each day. It would be like building an emotional wall around our hearts and not letting feelings enter.

In loving and being loved, we become most truly ourselves. Love is that strong of an emotion. It is that much a part of us. Love creates true joy. In the end, nothing we do or say in this lifetime will matter as much as how deeply we have loved. This last sentence defines how powerful love is and how important it is to expand your definition of this emotion so you can experience it more often.

Become more and more loving and you will become more and more joyful. It does not matter if it is a person, an animal, or a rock. Sit by a rock and have a chat. Stroke the rock and feel at one with it. The rock may not return anything, but that is not the point of love. You become joyful because you loved that rock. And if you can do this with a rock, it is easy to move on to sentient beings!

102. Find Ways to Enjoy Work

Many of us spend more waking hours at work than in our homes or with our spouse/families, so, clearly, it's very important to enjoy our work as much as possible. This doesn't mean that every workday has to feel like you're in paradise. Whatever job or career you choose will have its up and down moments. But, for the most part, you should experience more positive days at work than negative. If you follow your strengths and values in choosing your career, then you are more likely to find meaning through your work.

However, not everyone is in a position to do this. If you fall into this category, then it is important to understand how to find happiness in any task. This will allow you to find happiness and joy in your work.

One approach that seems to be successful most of the time is when you begin your next task at work, go at it with your whole heart. Find delight in doing the task. Even if you have completed this task a thousand times before, become so involved in it that it takes on new meaning. Pay close attention to the task, infusing it with awareness. In this one-pointedness, you can become wholehearted and focus on doing just that one thing. This does take effort, but you'll soon find that by following this technique, you will look at your job or career in a more positive light.

You can also engage with what you are doing in the spirit of service. You can look at your work as contributing to the well-being of others; see your job as a vehicle for spiritual and emotional growth. Depending on the type of career you have, this may have been one of the reasons you went into this field to begin with. Sometimes all it takes is reminding yourself of this. Think about how many people you can positively affect by the way you do your job.

Another technique is to see your work as a training step on the path toward what you really want to do. We live in an era of frequent job changes; we usually do not have the same job for our entire working career. So whether you are starting a new job in a new field, or trying to climb up in your present position, take pride in performing your job well, no matter what. Maybe you are paying your dues now for a brighter future. Show yourself and others what you are capable of.

When you go through this section, it is important to keep the following in mind: Work is empty without a personal life, and a personal life is lacking without fulfilling work. They sometimes pull you in opposite directions, but each supports the other. Mindfulness, moderation, and patience help you balance these complementary aspects of life.

103. Make Choices

Very rarely in life can you say you do not have a choice in a matter. We always have choices, if only to choose the meaning we take out of the circumstances we find ourselves in. The freedom of choice brings us happiness.

The future is formed by the choices you make. The future is not where you are going but what you are *creating*. The path is not something you find but something you *make*. This concept is based on your choices, and it's important to embrace them, whatever they may be. The happiness you thought was elusive is within your grasp when you recognize that you are not a victim of circumstances. The choices that truly happy people make explain how such joy-producing principles as intention, accountability, appreciation, and truthfulness can be applied in our daily lives to help us become happier.

Decisions can stir up powerful feelings. Keep in mind that your thoughts are just thoughts—they are not you, or reality. Which choices will benefit others? Which choices will benefit you? Which choices will move you toward peace? And, which choices will lead you to greater happiness?

104. Expand Your Happiness

If you are only happy when doing a limited number of things, or only happy when a certain person is around, or only happy when you are not working—then you are seriously missing out. Think of all the opportunities for happiness you are missing because of the limits you have imposed. Expanding your happiness repertoire is essential.

You can certainly understand how being overly picky about what brings you joy is preventing happiness from pervading your life. Sometimes people just do not have a plan and rely too much on others to make them happy. They need serious involvement in hobbies or activities, getting "out" of themselves and contributing to the world and to others. If you raise your children and then totally rely on talking to and seeing them as they get older, you will be disappointed. They have their own lives now and should not be obligated to fill up yours. By expanding what makes you happy, you eliminate this set of circumstances and create a better environment.

From childhood onward, we should cultivate hobbies and interests that are meaningful to us. Some people may want to participate in more social activities. Others may be more solitary and are happy doing these things on their own. No matter what your inclination is, you need to have hobbies and interests that fall into both areas, so you always have choices, so that when people aren't around to do things with you, you are fine, and when circumstances prevent one activity, you have another you can do.

It is our privilege and even duty to make something of our life, to create a diversified set of interests (not talking on the phone, shopping, watching television!) so we are constantly growing and learning throughout life. Change is inevitable, so you need to roll with that. Something you were deeply interested in as a child may no longer fascinate you. Find things to expand your happiness repertoire—creative ventures, physical activity, community service projects—the sky's the limit.

105. Help Others

Doing things for others helps you get out of yourself, but doing things for others with expectation of thanks or reward or recognition is not the same thing. Giving a gift to someone when it's all tied up in your desire for them to think you're great is not an unselfish and thoughtful gift. Helping someone with the hope of accolades is not a kindness at all. You don't find happiness this way.

We focus too much on ourselves. Practicing true generosity is an impulse of the heart, and is guided by awareness. It is a giving that is not dictated by a sense of guilt, by a debt, by wanting to show off or create dependence. It is truly a free gift, which in itself generates freedom. This feeling even exists when you are generous to yourself.

You can be generous by offering attention and thought, like a competent view or a brilliant idea or a suggestion of possibilities. Studies have found that happier people tend to be more generous. If you are more content, you are likely to be kinder to others. Someone who is gratified is more apt to feel generous and to help another in difficulty. Generosity is a mood lifter.

We all have the potential to be generous, to give that which is dearest to us. After an act of generosity, we may be poorer, but we will feel richer. It's an act that transforms us. We will also have made the world we live in a little kinder. Every day is filled with opportunities to be generous. Knowing the power of a generous heart, offer compliments, give accurate feedback, listen carefully. You cannot lose by being generous.

106. Develop a Sense of Belonging

The sense of belonging is a basic need and part of the answer to the eternal question: Who am I? You belong to a family, a group, a society, and a profession, and these affiliations define you and give you reasons for existing. Without this sense of belonging, you would feel like nothing. We come to know who we are by our reference to others. It is a basic need, like that for food and shelter.

We live in an era of individualism and in a society that celebrates being special and creative. This is not always a good thing, as many people use this to compete with and critique others. Individuality used to be less important. Even though a sense of community and belonging was more valued in the past, that doesn't mean it's any less important today. We need to cultivate it. Anything we can do to strengthen community and move away from isolation is worthwhile. I use a sports analogy to explain this better: Think of the best sports team you know of. What the players all have in common is the fact that they function as a team. Each player makes the other players better. It takes the entire team functioning at a high level to perform well.

One step in the right direction is to be free and flexible in our definition of belonging. Knowing that all human beings seek happiness, you can look upon them with more openness and empathy and kindness. You can work toward making yourself and others feel more included.

The longing to be connected to others still lives in us. It does not matter where you find a social or spiritual group to be a part of—on the Internet, in your town, in your church, or across the globe. You can start with your interests and beliefs and go from there. The experience of community can be nurtured. Opportunities for making others feel included come along regularly. We can include others as we develop our own sense of belonging.

107. Make Someone Else Happy

Okay, you can't really *make* someone else happy; it is his or her choice. But certainly you know how to be kind to your family, friends, and coworkers and add to their happiness. One of the best ways to feel happier yourself is to look for simple ways to bring joy to others.

There is an upwelling of the heart when you increase someone else's happiness. You can call it *sympathetic joy*. Wanting to bring happiness to someone else feels good; that's what random acts of kindness are all about.

Right now, you can come up with at least five ways to bring happiness to every person close to you. Making lists like this is one way to start. Then decide to do an act of kindness every day for a week, perhaps choosing a different person each day.

Opportunities for kindness are all around us. It's a matter of paying attention, focusing on the well-being of others. We are all connected to one another, and we all react to what happens on our planet. Each person is the whole world. If you can bring some relief and a sense of well-being to just one person, you've made a start toward relieving the suffering and pain in the world.

108. Relish What You Have

Relishing what you have is a way to promote more gratitude, and thereby happiness, in your life. So, relish what you have! Use the gift of your senses to thoroughly enjoy the things that make you happy, even the really tiny things. This appreciation, in the moment, makes it easier, too, to detach from items and happenings. If you appreciate them when you have them, then when things change or you lose them, you will be okay.

Really enjoying what you have helps you celebrate the abundance in your life. It fills you with happiness, not longing for something more or something different. There will always be those who appear to have more things, more money, a better job than you. You do not have control over that. But you *do* have control over relishing what you have.

Appreciate good times. It is easy in good times to respond, not react. Whatever you cultivate during these good times gives you strength for later, when things may change. Difficulties arise in both good and bad situations, and you can be ready to respond wisely in both.

Relish the people in your life, both family members and friends. Appreciate how important these relationships are to you. Relishing what you have in life promotes gratitude and, therefore, happiness.

109. Celebrate

Take celebrations to the next level. Instead of just celebrating birthdays and holidays, celebrate everything. When you finish something, celebrate! When you find something you have been looking for, celebrate! Take every opportunity you can to celebrate good things that happen in your life.

Celebrate how far you've come, how much you've learned, the joy of the every day, being alive, breathing . . . everything!

Celebrate each month, each season, each holiday, in whatever way you want! Celebrate surviving the dental appointment, getting an e-mail from someone who typically doesn't respond, or seeing a double rainbow! Make celebration an art.

110. Listen to Intuition and Impulses

One way to obtain lasting happiness is to acquire self-knowledge. By looking inward, you discover your strengths and talents. You need to be fully aware of your good points so you can develop the courage to deal with your weaknesses and bad points.

When you know yourself well, you are free to move forward. Inner intelligence deepens your experience and gives your life greater richness and meaning. This means listening to your intuition. You've heard that your first instinct about the right answer on a multiple-choice test is usually the right answer. Your other intuitions work that way, too.

Your intuition guides your soul the way your other five senses teach you about what is outside of you. Developing mindfulness makes you more self-aware. You need to listen to others, but also to yourself.

Self-awareness increases your self-confidence. You may not understand what is behind a hunch or an impulse. Mindfulness lets you study motivation and intention. Instead of immediately acting on a hunch or ignoring an impulse, do a mindfulness practice or meditation. Listen to and analyze your impulses, and examine and consider following these clues and leads.

111. Center Yourself

It is very important to center yourself in life. *Centering* is the concept of being in the calm and peaceful space that is always within you. It is important that you stay in the space as much as you can throughout your day, no matter what is going on in your life. When you are not centered, you will be unclear and unfocused. You will be stressed and off-balance. However, when you are centered, you will experience a state of clarity, focus, and peace. Without a center you can do routine things, but you will never be creative. Centering allows you to live at the maximum, at the peak.

You could choose a sacred word as a symbol in a centering prayer. Sit quietly and silently introduce the sacred word. When your mind wanders, gently come back to the centering prayer. As with all forms of meditation, it does take practice. But each time you do this, you will become better at it and become more aware of the positive results you will experience as a result.

Bring awareness to walking wherever you are. Slow down a bit, centering yourself in the present moment in your body. Appreciate the fact that you are able to walk. This is not something to take for granted. Walk with dignity and confidence. As Lao Tzu said, "Just remain in the center, watching. And then forget that you are there."

You can also do a standing centering meditation. It begins with a physical movement of your body to actually feel yourself physically centering. Lean forward a bit, then backwards, then left, then right. You will be leaning only an inch or two each way. Rest in a spot that feels balanced, in complete equilibrium. Think of the very center of your being as the center of a cyclone or tornado. Whatever happens around it does not affect it. It is eternal silence and calm. This silence brings truth and love and blessings to you.

112. Define Yourself

Write down ten words that define you. Why? These ten words can help you be true to yourself in your life choices, bringing greater happiness. This is similar to any "Who am I?" exercise. Do you assume that you know who you are? Before solving the problems in your life, spend some time with the fundamental question, "Who am I?"

The basic "Who am I?" exercise involves asking the question and then responding to myriad answers. If a name seems to be the answer, inwardly reply, "No, that is a name I have given myself. Who is the I who I gave that name to?" If it is felt or perceived, as in "I am the person who feels tired," the reply is "No, that is just a sensation I feel. Who is the I who has that sensation?" All of the answers that arise are responded to in this way. After each response there is an active, dynamic search for the next answer. Continue to reject the previous answer and search for the next answer in order to reject and go past it. The answers themselves do not matter; they are part of a deepening process of understanding yourself.

Your ten defining words help you stay mindful of what you love, cherish, and hold dear. These are very revealing words. This list can be expanded by writing down twenty-five more words for each one of your ten words. Without thinking too much about it, just do word association—the twenty-five words that first come to mind when you consider the first ten.

This inner knowledge of what defines you will help you concentrate on what makes you happiest.

113. Cultivate Energy

The best way to increase your energy is to find lots of things to be enthusiastic and happy about. For you it might be having a clean house, going out to dinner a couple of times a week, a pet who gives you unconditional love, or going to the gym. There are literally millions of opportunities for you to become excited and thoroughly enjoy what you do. The most difficult part about doing this exercise is to begin it. Once you start it, your enthusiasm takes over and you find happiness in the activity itself.

Complaining or worrying takes energy away from you. Working and playing hard give you more energy. The more things you plan to do, the more energy you'll have. If you are doing things you are enthusiastic about, you know you'll have a chance for flow experiences and happy moments. You know you get nothing from complaining and worrying. We were not put in this world to complain or worry, to cause problems or harm. We were put here to appreciate, to be kind and generous, and to create happiness.

Give each moment your full attention and awareness. The excitement of being alive will fill you. The world owes you nothing, but you owe the world gratitude for your life. Each moment should be a tribute to this gratitude.

Don't waste energy battling all the little waves; the ocean is full of them, and they just keep on coming. Simply pay attention and correct the course when necessary.

114. Deal with Things Constructively

We each have to figure out ways to deal with things that go wrong. Some people find that it helps to be with friends or family. Others feel better listening to music or creating artwork. Instead of sulking or moping, it is better to find a healing activity. What works for you is very personal.

Sometimes it is best to do normal things, things you like doing, when times are tough. You feel comfortable in your routines, and this connects you to your "happier self." Being relaxed and at ease will often help you figure out a constructive solution to your problem.

Nature is a powerful force. Being outside, enjoying nature, is often very helpful when dealing with a depressing situation. Nature gives you perspective and is a positive inspiration.

Another constructive way to deal is to do physical activity: exercising, gardening, walking, cooking or baking, cleaning. These activities, when you are mindful and enthusiastic, can put you in a flow, truly removing your focus from pain and suffering. You are in the moment of the physical activity, only.

You can also choose to spend time with happy people. Being alone may be your instinct, but this often breeds sulking and moping. Being around a happy person can be beneficial, even productive. The challenge is to face the suffering, remain kind, and get through the difficulty.

115. Live Each Day

You have heard this many times, but only because it is so true. You can live today as though it was your first and your last. Greet the day with a smile; see the day as a gift. You are alive.

What should you choose to do to bring more meaning and purpose into your life on this day? What should you think and do to make yourself and others smile, feel joy, and be happy? How can you make the world a better place because you have this day to live?

As you wake up, welcome the new day with a mindful smile for each breath you take. Ask that you may live each moment with compassion and awareness. Ask that you may walk on a path of peace and do no harm. Ask that you become more aware. Each day, spend some time in quiet contemplation of your own wealth of knowledge and talents.

Make a list of the most important activities you need to complete each day to be successful. Now, close your eyes and visualize yourself entering into a state of mindfulness as you undertake and complete each activity. In this way, you can live each day to the fullest.

116. Keep Art around You

The art on your walls and in galleries and museums does not just happen. And real art is not limited to those pieces created by famous artists. Open your eyes! Everything around you can be looked at as art. Nature and landscape are great pieces of art that can offer much enjoyment. You can see great works of art in your imagination, or in the pages of books.

The art around you encompasses two areas. The first is the art that you can look at. It is important to have art that you like in your environment, both at home and at work. If you choose carefully, works of art that you invest in will last for years and years. Framed pictures can be regularly refreshed. Fresh flowers are also art, even the bouquets sold at the grocery store. The definition of art is very wide. It can be defined as whatever you like to look at.

The second element of art around you is art that you create. If you like to paint, you can create art to decorate many of your rooms. It takes time and confidence, but many of us can release our inner artist onto canvas or paper. This is an inexpensive way to pursue a hobby and decorate. Ceramics, knitting, and weaving are also ways to express yourself artistically. Bring concentration, effort, and patience to the artwork. Enter into this activity without judgment, simply be present and fully aware of what you are doing. Be grateful for the ability to create a drawing or painting, or whatever you define as art.

117. Give Yourself the Gift of Light

There is something to be said for going green and conserving electricity. Whenever possible, we should try to conserve energy. But darkness is depressing, and you should give yourself the gift of as much light as possible. The human body is designed to absorb light. It needs it in order to survive and to create a sense of well-being.

You can add more light to your environment with the thoughtful selection of window treatments, like curtains and blinds. Skylights or sunrooms offer us free sunlight. Be generous with your lighting.

Invite it in from the outside. Make sure lights are on in the room you are in. Make sure you have appropriate lights for reading and other activities. Full-spectrum lighting is an efficient and pleasant alternative to regular incandescent bulbs for reading. And spending even fifteen minutes each day outside in the sunlight is a great help in achieving more happiness.

Lights cheer and welcome us, illuminating our home and desk, illuminating things we love. Your activities go more smoothly and are more cheerful when the area is well lit. Light can provide comfort when you are performing many tasks.

Light comes in many forms. When bright light is not needed, sometimes softer light can provide a positive and healthy environment. Candles offer soft, warm illumination. Lighting a candle brightens both the room and the lives of those who enjoy that candle. Light the candle mindfully and shine the light of awareness. This is a reminder that the sole purpose of human existence is to kindle a light in the darkness of mere survival.

118. Keep Happy Colors Around You

The colors around you and the colors you expose yourself to increase your happiness. What you wear, how you decorate, what you notice around you—you are sensitive to the different energies and effects of these colors. Colors play an important role in your life. By being aware of the impact colors have on you, you can create an environment that is rich, healthy, and conducive to happiness.

The colors of nature, like blue sky and green grass, beautiful flowers, fresh fruits and vegetables, all impact us. Look at nature whenever you get a chance and feel how the different colors affect you. Become aware of the impact.

When you visualize scenes, they are always in color. The colors you wear both reflect and influence your mood. We could all become happier with more cheerful colors in our lives. When you shop, whether it is for clothes, food, or decorations, be adventurous with color. Add colors that you don't already have around you. Experiment with new combinations of colors.

Study the colors you are drawn to, and the color combinations you love. Train your eyes to look and really see the subtle differences in tints and shades of the rainbow. Find out what colors give you pleasure and energy. A good way to do this is to collect the paint color chips at the paint or hardware store that are your favorites. Then you can figure out the associations you have with the different colors you chose. You will see your own personal color palette emerge.

Meditating on different colors is a useful way of strengthening your visualization skills. How does the energy of each feel? How does each color affect your emotions? When you have finished, take some deep breaths and open your eyes. Visualize a color in your mind's eye, in all of its depth and richness, while reflecting on and trying to assume the color's positive qualities.

119. Practice Introspection

Introspection is underrated. Introspection is the contemplation of your own thoughts and desires and conduct. Tuning in to your thoughts, feelings, and sensations is part of meditation. Knowing more about yourself makes it easier to deal with life and improve your ability to care for yourself and others. Introspection can make you more compassionate, kind, and loving.

Living in an ever-changing world, we often feel that we're being tossed around like a boat in a stormy sea. With insight meditation and introspection, you may be able to see more clearly. This type of reflection sheds light on your internal life, thereby making things clearer when you look outward. Insight meditation focuses on the natural passing of all events within the mind and the body. Beginning with the focusing of attention on the breath, the practice concentrates and calms the mind. It allows one to see through the mind's conditioning and thereby to live more fully present in the moment.

Also, stop from time to time during the day and pay attention to your inner dialogue. You are not your thoughts, and you need to get used to not always believing the messages they send. But when you have a concern or doubt, listen to your inner voice, your heart. It is a fine line, but worth investigating. If you go through life on auto-pilot, you don't know yourself. If you spend too much time in your head, ruminating, you don't take action or have any peace.

Practice letting go and soon you will be able to cultivate inner peace. Take a step toward inner peace by accepting whatever is happening in the present moment. Silently say "yes" to your feelings and thoughts, sensations within your body, sights you see, and sounds you hear. Allow what *is* to simply be there, without wishing it to change in any way.

120. Say No

Saying that you are not able to do something, that you have a conflict, that it's not a good time—when done sincerely—is being respectful of yourself. Many of us need to train ourselves how to say "no" nicely and definitively.

There are times when saying "no" is appropriate. We need to value our own plans and projects, just as much as we need to respect others'. Say "no" consciously, politely. And respect the wishes of others when they say "no." Just like you don't want people to take it personally when you say "no," don't take it personally when people say "no" to you. Thank them for being honest.

There are other things we say "no" to because we always have, or because saying "yes" scares us. For ten minutes, notice the ways your mind keeps saying "no" to life or certain activities, suppressing your feelings and impulses, judging or rejecting other people, refusing to accept things the way they are. Then, for ten minutes, just say "yes". Whatever you experience, whomever you meet, however life presents itself to you, note your tendency to resist or deny and instead, say "yes". Experiment. Say "yes" to your feelings, your partner or kids, your body, your face, and your life. Repeat the word "yes" to help get you started.

121. Practice Single-Object Meditation

Single-object meditation is a great way to bring more happiness into your life because you are focusing your mind on just one object. The number of signals sent to your brain is greatly reduced, allowing your mind to settle down into a deeply relaxed, yet highly alert state.

When you try this form of meditation, start by concentrating on a particular object. Feel its presence and focus on its texture, shape, or other qualities. A crystal, candle flame, flower, mandala, etc., are all suitable objects.

Meditate on this one object, looking at it actively, dynamically, alertly, but without words. Once you've chosen your object (i.e., a flower), look at it as if you were feeling it.

Another concept of single-object meditation is to imagine that you are a single drop of water in the sea. Together with billions of other drops, you form an ocean. Meditate upon your spirit, one among many, but part of One.

Utter *Om* as a single attenuated note, like "Ah-ohhhhhhmmmmmm." You may chant this mantra, or combine it with other words at the beginning and ending of a prayer, such as "Om, Shanti," which means "peace."

122. Change Your Commute

Are you sick of your daily commute? Maybe what seemed like a reasonable distance a few years ago has become a longer journey due to increased traffic. If you calculate your time on the road each year, you may shudder.

Some people love their time in the car because it allows them to "shift gears" between work and home; others don't. If you would like to reclaim some of that time for your personal life, think of different ways of doing so. There are many creative ways to reduce your commute. Many companies are open to new ideas to keep their employees happy, efficient, and productive. Perhaps you could telecommute, or work at home for one day a week. You could move nearer to your workplace, or find a job nearer your home. You could carpool with someone so you have company on the road. You could use traveling time for listening to audiobooks, podcasts, or favorite music.

A simple starting point for converting your commute from tedious to energizing is to employ slow, deep breathing. Sit up straight, as if a string were pulling your head up to the sky. You will be doing normal, diaphragmatic breathing. Hold the inhaled breath for the same amount of time it took to breathe in, then exhale on that same count a third time. For example, if you inhale on a four count, hold for four, and then exhale the full breath on four beats. For a stressed driver, it doesn't mean you have to maintain breath awareness during the whole commute, but it does mean remembering to perform the exercise periodically and consistently while you are commuting.

When you see a red light or a stop sign, smile at it and thank it because it helps you return to the present moment and mindfulness. See it as a friend, helping you to resist rushing. The light or sign says: Stop, return to the present moment. Ask that you meet the present moment with joy and peace. Breathe and smile. Remember that the car acts as your legs. It goes where you choose. When you drive with awareness, everyone lives in safety.

123. Get Better or More Sleep

Tiredness makes us more vulnerable and less able to cope or see the positives when life is not running smoothly. It is harder to keep your sense of humor and to feel happy when you are tired than it is when you are full of energy. Many people suffer from sleeping problems or have a snoring partner, so trying various methods to get a good night's sleep is important.

There are some steps we can take to try to help ourselves get a good night's sleep. Treat your bedroom as a haven. Decorate it in an inspiring way and have green plants if you can, because they add moisture and oxygen. Since this is where you sleep, don't work in the room if you can avoid it. If you have room for a chair, sit there if you want to read, listen to music, or do other activities, instead of sitting on the bed.

Make sure your day includes exercise. Try to stick with a regular sleeping pattern with set bedtimes and wake-up times. Eat dinner earlier so you have plenty of time to digest your food, and avoid dessert or snacks in the evening. Drink decaffeinated beverages or milk products if you must have something to drink after dinner.

There are many herbs and essential oils that are calming and offer a natural sleep remedy when used on the skin, in a diffuser, in a candle, etc. An eye pillow or body lotion with lavender works for many people.

Meditating before you go to bed often helps in getting the mind to settle down. There are many techniques to try, including this: As you go to bed and prepare for sleep, take some mindful breaths, become aware of the bed supporting you, and allow yourself to smile. Take a moment to be thankful for a night of safety and a warm, dry place to sleep. Feel the muscles of your body relaxing as you sink into your bed.

124. Learn a New Skill

Research on happiness suggests that enduring happiness comes from finding opportunities to develop new skills. These challenges differ depending on the stage of your life. At one stage in your life, you might opt for flying lessons or running a marathon. At another stage in your life, you might choose to learn how to play a musical instrument or how to weave rugs.

When you begin to learn new skills, the most important things are attitude and opportunity. You may never have had the opportunity to learn something when you were in your twenties, but later on in life, when you find you have more time and fewer responsibilities, or your financial situation is different, you can try it. Don't let age or social conventions hold you back!

Most of us want to add more challenge and learning to our lives. Few people want no change, or for everything to be too easy, routine, and dull. The challenge of acquiring new skills and abilities, with all the inherent difficulties, is worthwhile. Sometimes the fact that something is hard—requiring real effort and the overcoming of obstacles—is what gives you a huge amount of happiness, especially when you triumphantly reach your goal.

Sometimes learning something new can be inspirational and enjoyable in its own right. It does not have to have a particular point or purpose. There are opportunities everywhere for learning new skills. Night classes, weekend classes, distance learning, part-time courses, reading something different, renting documentaries, listening to podcasts or radio programs discussing subjects of interest—these are all ways to increase knowledge and be humbled by what you don't know. As you add to the list of things you can do today that you could not do last year, you will grow in confidence. You will also discard habits that no longer serve any useful purpose, and you will become more of the person you want to be.

125. Increase Comedy and Humor in Your Life

The power of laughter brings an instant feel-good factor into your life. Remember the times when you laughed uncontrollably. People love to laugh, and everyone finds humor in different situations. Certainly what is funny to one person may very well not be funny to another, but most people agree that the most popular comedy films and television shows are funny. There appears to be a common denominator. Think of Monty Python, the Marx Brothers, Lucille Ball's *I Love Lucy*, Peter Sellers's *The Pink Panther*, and the Mel Brooks movies. These programs and movies captured huge audiences because of their ability to make people laugh.

Jokes are spread by word of mouth, phones and the Internet, and television and radio. The objective is to make people laugh, temporarily forgetting their problems and releasing the pressures of everyday life. Whatever the source and whatever the delivery, humor is often the key to lifting spirits and creating happiness.

Here are some steps that you can take to increase the laughter and humor in your life:

- *Choose to have a healthy sense of humor.*
- *Use gentleness and a sense of humor to settle down and stay present.*
- *When you laugh, laugh through your whole body. Feel laughter coming from the very soles of your feet. At first, you might not be able to feel if it is happening or not, but it will. Just keep at it, and soon laughter will actually start in your feet and move upward.*
- *Try to laugh at more things. Even try laughing at yourself for some of the things you do.*
- *Take time to laugh. For seven days, begin by shouting "YAA-HOO" a few times, and then just laugh for no reason at all for twenty minutes, either sitting or lying down. Let go. At the end, just sit and let go and enjoy yourself.*

126. Relax

Relaxation is very important for our minds and bodies. Just like recharging a battery, relaxation recharges us. It is necessary to put aside some time each day to relax. As you practice the art of relaxation, you will find that you can begin to turn it on and off like a switch. You are in control of the relaxation process.

127. Control Your Money

Money is one of those difficult things to think about because it is so complex. It seems so much of life revolves around money. But money does not buy you happiness. Start out with these helpful hints:

- *Keep yourself to one or two credit cards, with low credit limits.*
- *Practice self-restraint. Ask yourself before buying something: Do I really need this? Do I have to spend this money? What other choices do I have? What could I do instead?*
- *Make it a priority to pay off your debts and keep to a budget.*
- *Try a daily/weekly spending log so you get an idea of what you are doing, the way you would have a food diary to get an idea of what you are eating.*
- *Set a time each month to pay bills.*
- *Look into ways to get the best deals, like a better type of mortgage.*
- *Regularly examine your assets and make sure you are using them wisely.*
- *Get advice from an expert or experts if you need it.*

Remember, you possess your money—it does not possess you. Money can be helpful or harmful, can further either good or evil, depending on whether you use it or abuse it.

Deal with the fluctuations of material life. Stay content and steady during the financial ups and downs of life. If you have less money, lower your wants. If you have more money, use what you have to benefit others—or save it!

128. Let Go of Expectations

Each of us has a set of values and beliefs that is personal and formed by many factors. When other people do things that do not fit with our values and beliefs, we can get angry, disappointed, frustrated, or upset. We often expect other people to say or do things that we would say or do ourselves. When they don't, our negative feelings detract from our potential for happiness. This is what happens when you have expectations for what others should believe and value.

Think about the times when your values and beliefs differed from others'. Have you been disappointed and unhappy when a loved one did not telephone you? Have you ever discovered that someone you care about does not have the same view of honesty that you have? How do you respond if a family member does not clean up after themselves? What happens if someone cuts you off on the road? What happens when someone does not agree with your political or spiritual beliefs?

You are getting the point here that these expectations of yours have and are causing you and people around you some upset. Can you see that other people are not within your control? You (and they) will fare better if you find a way to let go and not let your expectations push negative feelings to take over. Respecting that others have different values and beliefs is the starting point.

Now look at some other steps you can take to continue to let go of expectations. How can you respect that others have a different set of values or beliefs from yours? How much better would it be if you let your negative feelings go? Think of a person or situation about which you feel anger or anguish or bitterness or regret. Hold that image and look at it from every angle. Focus on your role in this: Where were you wrong or thoughtless or mistaken? Imagine how you would feel if you were no longer angry or upset at the person or situation. Explore the possibility of making amends, offering forgiveness, or simply letting go of your resentment. Then, make the amend. Offer forgiveness. Let go. Make a commitment to not harbor resentments in the future.

129. Know Your Purpose

Some lucky people have always known what they wanted out of life. They have a natural vocation or calling. They know what they want to do and enjoy doing it. These people are the minority. Many others keep looking and hoping that what they want to do will spring out of their current activities, or lightning will strike and they will suddenly know. Many students still go to college without knowing what they want to do when they graduate. Others continue in jobs and careers that are not suitable or enjoyable for them. Much time is wasted when you use this approach.

Yet most people spend a huge amount of their lives at work. They focus on the weekends and vacations and go to work as part of a routine. They do not get any real pleasure from it. Anything you can do to discover your purpose would move you away from this type of life, where you're just working to pay the bills.

Happy people find a work-and-life balance. They derive as much pleasure from life at work as they do from life at home. What can you do to discover your purpose? You need to do whatever you can to circumvent the "When I'm ____ / when I have ____, I'll be happy." That means you see happiness as something outside yourself and out of your control. Though achieving some goals that fill in those blanks may bring some degree of happiness, there is no guarantee that they will bring long-term satisfaction unless they are in line with your overall sense of purpose.

First, remember that you can have happiness anytime, anyplace, and anywhere. Happiness is a state. You don't have to wait for it or leave it to chance. You can have happiness now; it is within you. It is much easier to believe this if you feel you are playing a worthwhile part in the destiny of the universe. So, start looking for your deeper meaning and purpose. Get involved with charities, religion, spirituality. Discover your strengths, get schooled, get a job you love. Having a deeper purpose brings you increased motivation, energy, and, ultimately, happiness.

130. Practice Seed Meditation

Use seed meditation to bring a fresh outlook to any problem or issue. Take a blank sheet of paper. In the center, write the word or phrase, the *seed* you are focusing on. Maybe it is an issue that is causing you problems (money, teenager), or a character trait that you'd like to cultivate (patience, tolerance). Circle the word or phrase, then close your eyes and hold the word or phrase in your mind.

When associations arise, however odd, write them down, circle them, and link them to the seed word or phrase with a line. Between each burst of uncensored brief writing, you close your eyes and go back inside. You relax and let go, allowing your mind to create these associations.

Whether you choose to end the seed meditation when the page is filled, or to put a time limit on it (like a half-hour), eventually the page will be covered with inner associations. Like journal writing, this is an opportunity to let things out on paper and quiet your judgmental mind. This opens you to more spacious and fruitful ways of thinking.

Repeat this meditation as many times as you like, using the same seed. Gradually your powers of thinking will wake up and your awareness will let you see the situation differently. You will observe your thoughts and realize that you are not your thoughts. You will see your inner world differently.

131. Make a List of What's Right about You

It's easy to overlook what others appreciate about you, or to discount and dismiss what you could appreciate more about yourself. This is very common for us to do. Making a "What's Right About Me" list will help you become aware of your strengths in a way that may be helpful in bad times, when you tend to be unkind to yourself.

What's "right" about you will include your talents and strengths, your physical capabilities, your psychological gifts, but also some more subtle qualities. You may be the person who people turn to when they don't know how to spell something. You may be the one who is able to come up with a useful strategy in an office crisis.

Maybe you are the one who can whip up a whole meal in twenty minutes.

If you are not sure what is "right" about you, you can try this variation on seed meditation. In the center of a blank piece of paper, put your name and also the name of someone who knows and appreciates you. Thinking about yourself from this person's perspective, write down all the qualities that this person can see and appreciate in you.

Follow the seed meditation process by writing spontaneously, without censoring yourself. Close your eyes, reflect, and then write again. Do this for at least twenty minutes. You may do more seed meditations using other people from different areas of your life. Making a list or lists like this can make you more appreciative of yourself and others.

132. Make a List of What Went Right Today

This exercise encourages you to be positive about each and every day. First, when you are around others, take care that you talk about what went well that day, what you appreciated and enjoyed, and what you found stimulating, amusing, or touching. Let the negatives of the day go. Don't complain. Be positive. This prepares your mind for your "What Went Right" list.

When you begin this list, concentrate on the small details. It is very often the little things that "make our day." What were the little things you noticed and the things that went right today? It is always good to stop and smell the roses. Making a list of the things that made you feel happy is often harder than rattling off the things that went wrong or that worry you. Why is that? Because we dwell too much on the negative, trying to "understand" or "figure it out," not following the simple rule that if you can't do something about it, let it go.

Yes, this is hard to do. However, if you turn this exercise into a habit, it will point you in the other direction. You will find that each day, you will pick up the positive more easily, and later, you'll remember it more readily. It helps when you compare your life with current media coverage. If you believe the media, more bad happens than good. Just look at all the negative articles in the newspaper and segments on the news. If you believe your thoughts, which naturally dwell on the bad, more bad happens than good.

This exercise is a "retraining" of your mind. You will begin to focus on what went right. Remember: You think—but you are not your thoughts. You can choose to focus on the positive and let the negative go.

133. Practice Ocean Meditation

When the world gets crazy and it seems that you are being pulled in a million different directions at once, you may need to incorporate stillness into your life. When this happens to me, I use an ocean meditation. Imagine the blue green ocean, sand along its edge, water swirling up to it. Your thoughts are the particles of sand, getting pulled into the ocean by the waves lapping the shore. The sand (your thoughts) float down and then settle on the ocean floor.

Let go of those thoughts as they settle down on the ocean floor, giving you the rest you need.

Let your awareness expand. Continue to watch the ocean's water. See how calm it becomes. When it is completely still, sunlight strikes it and lights everything.

You can also imagine that you are a single drop of water in the sea. Together with billions of other drops, you form an ocean. Meditate upon your spirit, one among many, but part of One. Feel the stillness settling in your mind.

134. Appreciate Your Body

You can learn to love your body. Your body is not something to complain about, control, manipulate, or torment. Many of us have, since adolescence, cultivated an ingratitude toward our bodies. We focus on perceived deficiencies, defects, and faults—comparing them to absurd notions of physical beauty that have little to do with good health, ease, and physical strength. You need to accept and love your body in order to have good health and happiness.

Take time to appreciate what is precious and alive about your body, no matter how far from an "ideal" your body shape may be. Be aware of how your attitude toward your body reflects your gratitude for life. Value the health and strength you have.

Be aware that there is no meaningful distinction between mind and body. Exercise both your body and your mind. Treat them as two aspects of the same whole. Explore treats you could give your body on a daily basis: the best and most nourishing food, adequate rest, fresh air, and mind/body exercise, like walking or yoga.

Focus on peace of mind, which supports your physical existence. Intention allows synapses to connect, and many hundreds and thousands of movements are carried out by your body each day. Appreciate the beauty of this system and what it allows you to do and experience.

135. Ask Yourself, Is This Kind?

If you behave in ways that cause you shame or leave you feeling anxious, disconnected, or empty, you can use a simple method to reconnect you with a more appreciative and loving self. The question is: Is this kind? When the answer is "no," you must take definitive action. Allowing kindness to guide what you do, say, and think will help you become much happier.

Ask yourself before you speak: *Is it true? Is it kind? Is it beneficial? Does it harm anyone? Is this the right time to say anything? Does what I am about to say improve upon silence?*

Essentially, this is the Golden Rule: Do unto others as you would have them do unto you. If you are kind to others, that kindness will come back to you, multiplied—but not always from the same people. If you are kind to someone, he or she feels inspired to be kind to another, and so on, and so on. In this way, you spread kindness from person to person.

This can be applied to deeds, also. It is important to understand that kind words or actions are their own reward. As you practice this more and more, you will see that you are able to apply this to your own thoughts. Your thoughts are involved in karma, too; they don't escape. Even your smallest, least significant thought, word, or action has real consequences throughout the universe.

136. Write Your Way Out of a Rut

When you feel life is not going your way or you feel overwhelmed by things, you can often feel like you're in a rut. It happens to everyone from time to time. When you experience this, it can be very helpful to write your way out of the rut. It does not have to be professional-quality writing; that's not the purpose here. It just has to come from your heart.

There are several ways to accomplish this exercise. You can utilize seed meditation (page 147) to deepen your awareness and write your way out of the rut. Or, another way of coping is to do free, expressive writing in a journal to get everything out, possibly freeing yourself of the problem. If this feeling lasts for a while, it gives you time to try and come up with something constructive to do about it.

The first step in breaking out of a rut is to see it for what it is. Patterns that are created very early in life continue until we become aware of them. One way to become aware of our deeply embedded patterns is to write our life story. Through reflective writing, you can tap into your subconscious, not just to identify the habits that hold you back, but also to rediscover long-buried gifts that can help you embrace your wholeness: physically, emotionally, spiritually, socially, and intellectually.

If you were to sit down right now to compose your autobiography, it might feel like an overwhelming task. Remember to enjoy the "journey" of your writing. Take your time—maybe weeks or months—and focus yourself by using some or all of the following exercises and techniques:

- *Recall in great detail four or five positive childhood memories.*
- *Write detailed descriptions of your friends and family.*
- *Record your impressions of parents, siblings, grandparents, friends, neighbors, or anyone else you feel has played a key role in your life.*
- *List the ten most important transitions of your life, then write about each one. Think about what you learned about yourself and what qualities you gained during these pivotal times.*

It is very helpful to write your story, even if you never share it with anyone else.

137. Resolve Conflict and Problems

Shared values have the power to heal emotional wounds and reduce conflict. If you explicitly acknowledge what you and another person mutually value—your love for one another, your shared history, a commitment to a child—you are allowing shared values to support you. This offers a basis for looking together at something that may be causing you a conflict or problem.

When you try to resolve a conflict, use friendly, cooperative language; no need to yell and shout. As much as you can, listen. Decide to listen more and talk less. Try to open up to the other person's reality, since you already know your own. Be generous, too. Working through difficulties in a relationship with your spouse, family member, friend, or colleague by using shared values can deepen the relationship in a way that good times alone cannot. It is an opportunity for growth, for all parties involved.

There are always problems, but many are self-made, as is some pain and suffering. You can choose to eliminate all the problems that may never happen. This can radically liberate you. You can also ask yourself if the conflict or problem is something you can really do something about. When you can do something, bring to the situation your experience, insights, and values. Ask, *What is needed here?* and *How would a wise person deal with this situation?*

You can also decide not to add pain and suffering to a problem. Do not "beat up" on yourself or others. Pay attention to what is needed, take appropriate action, and see yourself as someone who can deal with the situation using your insights, strengths, and values. Do what you can and let go. You will be giving yourself the "present" of peace.

138. Follow a Path Toward Peace

Making peace and walking peacefully through life support your path to happiness. Without being at peace, happiness is almost impossible. It is easy to get mad and angry, to let your negative and hurtful emotions get the best of you. A path of peace requires awareness, restraint, and attention. Here are some steps to follow that will set you on this path toward peace:

- *See the good in other people. By training yourself to do this, you create a powerful energy within yourself.*
- *Your life is a gift. Enjoy that gift by treating yourself and others with respect.*

- *Protect the environment; nature is your true home.*
- *If you or someone else makes a mistake, give yourself or the other person the benefit of the doubt. Let it go and chalk it up to learning.*
- *Remove yourself from harm, and shield those who are vulnerable.*
- *Reduce violence in act, speech, and thought.*
- *Focus on kindness and embrace all the characteristics of one who cultivates kindness.*
- *Listen more, and with an open mind.*
- *Value community and cooperation.*
- *Practice forgiveness and tolerance.*
- *Offer encouragement.*
- *Understand karma and the impact you have on all interconnected beings with what you do, say, and think. Remember the unity of life and the universe.*

139. Observe Your Thoughts

Most people believe that they *are* their thoughts. An awful thought enters your mind and you think, *Wow, how could I think like that?* But you are not your thoughts. You need to understand how thoughts work so you can change unhelpful attitudes. This is something you must experience, not just read here. By observing your thoughts, you can become aware of them without identifying with them or getting caught up in them.

When you catch yourself thinking the same thought or collection of thoughts repeatedly, especially when they are affecting your mood or outlook in a negative way, take the time to watch them. You will see that your thoughts change constantly, like a monkey swinging from tree to tree. Your thoughts run on a continuous loop when you are anxious or preoccupied, with a constant repetition of the same thought or collection of thoughts. Stop at times and pay attention to your inner dialogue. Watch the thoughts like a tennis player watches the ball. Some of them are very subtle, so you will have to wait like a cat for a mouse.

When you observe your thoughts, you learn how to separate yourself from them and not get embroiled in them. They are not who you are. Those anxious and emotional thoughts drive your emotions; as you think, so you will feel. It is extremely useful (and brings happiness!) to distance yourself from thoughts that are feeding anxiety and negative emotions. If you ignore negative thoughts, that is aversion. If you wallow in them, that is not productive. Be the observer and you will be surprised how some situations change without your involvement and, at other times, solutions present themselves to you as the observer.

If you want to think and feel differently, meditation can greatly aid this exercise. Remember that your thoughts are not inevitable, that they are self-made, and that they affect mood—not the other way around. You are not your thoughts, and you need to get used to *not* believing the messages they give. See them, like clouds going by or train cars moving along. They are part of your "picture," but you don't have to fly up to the clouds or jump on the train. Letting go of negative thoughts is one of the best feelings in the world.

140. Stop Criticism

One of the meanings of the word *criticism* is "the act of passing severe judgment." Whether we are criticizing others or ourselves, most of the time we do not even realize we are doing it. It is a bad habit. Criticism can do much harm to ourselves and others. With awareness, you can stop criticizing and begin to appreciate a new happiness because of this accomplishment.

If you recognize that you criticize someone a lot, try this: Every day for an entire month, find at least one specific positive thing you can say to the person. Maybe you can offer encouragement, express gratitude, or give praise. Try taking an interest in the person's interests, showing respect and being willing to listen. If you hear yourself start to criticize, *stop*. Leave the room.

Only by being less critical will you break your habit of criticizing this person. At the beginning, it may be difficult or feel awkward to praise or express gratitude to someone you having been criticizing. This is normal. If it doesn't feel natural to praise the person yet, at least stop yourself when you start to say something negative. It's a start!

As you begin to understand yourself more, you will become more aware of your motivations. Your motive for criticizing is to get a result, to change things. The moment you are not looking for a result—not looking to criticize, evaluate, or conclude—then you can stop being critical, because you're not trying to control things anymore. Stopping criticism will improve your life as well as the lives of those you've been criticizing. Everyone will be much happier.

141. Pause

A simple, helpful exercise that you can do in almost any situation is the act of pausing. Many times, just a little pause is all we need to be happier. If you pause before you choose to say something, you may be able to stop yourself from passing judgment; or maybe you'll choose to say something positive, or, nothing at all. If you pause before you speak, you will listen more carefully. Next time you talk to someone, relish the pauses and also the trust flowing within the conversation.

Pausing before you do something works the same way. A pause can help remind you of your values; remind you to respect others; and remember that they, too, are seeking happiness. Pausing lets you put your best foot forward.

If you work at a computer for many hours, it can lead to fatigue and pain. So when you are at your computer, pause every now and then to follow your breathing and notice how you are sitting. If you are a bit tense, stretch your neck different ways, straighten your spine, and relax your body. During gaps in the flow of your work, come back to your breathing. Feel yourself being recharged and in better control of yourself.

Before picking up the ringing phone, pause for a moment and let it ring one more time. Let the full ring complete itself. Listen to it. Compose yourself.

If you are feeling anxious or stressed out, try this pausing exercise to help you out:

- *Begin by saying "stop" and pausing in the activity.*
- *Breathe slowly and deeply. As you exhale, imagine that time is expanding.*

- *Continue to do this, each time lengthening the out-breath.*
- *After a couple of minutes, resume what you were doing with a calmer mind.*

142. Feed Your Mind

Feeding your mind with good things is an important element that leads to greater happiness. You feed your mind just like you feed your body. Do not fill your mind with harmful or disturbing information. Just like you know it is unwise to eat junk food all the time, feeding your mind with harmful or disturbing information will also have a negative effect. Feed the mind good things as you feed your body with good food. You should be aware that what you take in from the media (newspapers, magazines, television) affects your karma, so please choose carefully when you partake in these activities.

Choose to feed your mind with reading and creative activities. Feed it by opening your eyes to the beauty and wonders of the world. Choose great sounds for it to hear. Feed your mind, too, by sleeping soundly or napping when you need to. What goes into your mind is as important as what comes out of it in actions and speech. Nourishing your mind feeds your soul.

Pay attention to what you are feeding your mind. When you read something, read it as if the story happened to you. Become part of the story. It is also important to be conscious of what you are watching on television. In today's world, it is almost impossible to give up television altogether. So, at least when you are watching television, be aware and conscious of what you are watching. Do not just zone out and then say, "What did I just watch?" Bring together a good mixture of ingredients to make a yummy life stew.

When you think about it, all of our thoughts and emotions are forms of energy that we send out like a radio broadcast. They permanently affect our environment. Some people radiate thoughts and feelings of love, while others may produce a kind of mental or emotional pollution. This is about keeping your own mind healthy, as well as respecting the world around you. The Buddha said, "All that we are is the result of what we have thought. The mind is everything. What we think we become."

143. Deal with Anger

Anger is a by-product of dealing with people. It's natural to sometimes feel anger toward a person because of something he or she has done to you, or because of a perceived slight or wrong. Sometimes it may be someone's personality that makes you angry. When you do experience anger, it is important that you understand that emotion. Here are some little hints for you to use when you feel anger: Pay attention to situations you may experience as especially difficult. Avoid people who drive you crazy. If a person who drives you crazy is someone you have to work with or see regularly, protect yourself by identifying the behaviors that get to you the most, and mentally practice detaching from them. If you can, let the person know what really bothers you (i.e., "I really don't like to be touched a lot").

In dealing successfully with anger, it helps to understand your own temperament. Do you get easily frustrated? Do people who you perceive as lazy drive you nuts? Do people who don't agree with you make you mad? Are you patient? After you begin to understand your temperament, then you can work toward developing non-reactiveness. One of the best things you can teach yourself is to walk away or start counting or take deep breaths. Just think of the last time you got angry with a spouse or a close friend. Think about how much better it would have turned out if you had simply walked away or chosen not to react to the situation. A good way to develop nonreactiveness is to watch the anger rise, then watch it fall.

Develop a flexibility of emotional response. In the face of anger, for example, practice generating compassion toward yourself and others. In the face of greed, practice generating gratitude for all that you have. When experiencing jealousy, try to find the feeling of rejoicing in the good fortune of another. When impatient, practice patience.

Anger is a strong emotion. It can destroy love and friendships. In closing this section, think about the following: When you feel angry, try not to center on the person who aroused this emotion. Let him or her be on the periphery. Become the anger and allow it to happen within. Do not rationalize. Do not say that the other person has created it. Feel the wound and be grateful to the other person for helping you recognize this. Your awareness will let you become the emotion. You will be relieved of it through this awareness.

144. Change How You See Others

Just as it helps to become more aware of yourself, it is also helpful to become more aware of others. How do you see others? (Not their physical aspects, but what's on the inside.) The more genuinely you can see other people as complex, evolving individuals who are full of contradictions, the more it will be possible for you to respond sensitively and appropriately.

Anger ruins joy, steals the goodness of your mind, and forces your mouth to say terrible things. Overcoming anger brings peace of mind, leads to a mind without regrets. If you overcome anger, you will be delightful and loved by all. One way to accomplish this is to push yourself to see the real person, not just an image or a behavior. Pause and say to yourself that this person is seeking happiness, too.

When you find yourself repeatedly angry in similar situations, ask yourself, *What can I learn from this?* When you allow someone or something to make you angry, you're showing how you let yourself be controlled by your expectations of how that person or situation should be. When you accept yourself, others, and situations for what they are, you become more effective in influencing them to change in the ways that you would like them to.

Practice loving-kindness by saying, "May I be filled with loving-kindness today. May I be well. May I be peaceful and at ease. May I be happy." Then repeat these wishes for the other person. "May <person's name> be filled with loving-kindness. May <person's name> be well. May <person's name> be peaceful and at ease. May <person's name> be happy." Repeat this loving-kindness practice day after day until you can do it in your mind every time you are around the other person.

145. Be Aware of Your Moods

Moods, driven by emotions and thoughts, powerfully affect how you feel about yourself and how others perceive you. Moods are real and have to be dealt with. People may forget exactly what you said or did, but they will remember your mood or behavior. When you are in the presence of another person, his or her mood is what you instinctively feel.

We underestimate our moods and how they affect others. You need to be considerate of others by first noticing the effect of your moods on other people. This moves you to take full responsibility for your moods, which can be a huge wake-up call. It can make a powerful difference in the way other people experience being around you. You need wise reflection and consideration when it comes to where your actions are leading.

Awareness of yourself is a central theme in finding a path toward increased happiness. Happiness and awareness go hand in hand. A major step in awareness is to be very watchful of your thoughts. They are subtle and dangerous. When you become aware of your thoughts, you will be surprised. The very phenomenon of observing your thoughts can actually change them. Then you must also become aware of your emotions, feelings, and moods. This is the most subtle layer and the most difficult, but if you can be aware of your thoughts, then you're on your way.

146. Give to Others

Giving to others without needing to receive something in return is a gratifying experience. It's a wonderful feeling to bring a smile to someone's face and to make a difference. There are thousands of (free) ways to give to others, such as:

• *accept differences and show tolerance; accept people as they are*

- *allow yourself to be fully present in the moment*
- *be courteous*
- *do not blame*
- *do not keep a tally of what's given or owed*
- *give more of your concern, interest, and time than is necessary*
- *give the benefit of the doubt*
- *let past hurts and mistakes go*
- *limit your requests*
- *listen without judging*
- *pay attention to what someone needs, not what you think he or she needs*
- *praise and encourage*
- *receive gracefully*
- *refuse to participate in hurtful gossip*
- *rejoice in others' happiness*
- *resist sulking and moping*
- *take an interest in others' interests*
- *talk about what is positive, stimulating, uplifting*
- *value qualities more than achievements*
- *value your strengths and talents, and share them*

On your road to happiness, look at ways you can give to others.

147. Bless Youer E-mail

Writing e-mails is second nature for most of us, and they are often written in haste. E-mails often take on a bit more added significance compared to words that we speak aloud. Somewhere between your intention and what the person reads and comprehends, there can be a painful gap. When you write an e-mail, or respond to one, you need to pause and ask yourself, *How will this be interpreted?*

E-mails can come back to haunt us. Few among us have mastered this medium, and we're only slowly realizing its dangers. The peril of being off-key is amplified by the temptation to hit send prematurely, before we've thought it over and have had a chance to ease up on that too-stiff tone, drop that bit of sarcasm, or improve the language. Writing is about listening to your inner voice, not just composing meaningful sentences. Your writing can become a meditation.

Next time you are about to send an important e-mail or letter, try this: As you are about to hit the SEND button or put the letter into the mailbox, stop for a moment. Pause and align yourself with present-moment awareness. Feel the grace of the present moment and bless your e-mail or letter. Then hit send or put the letter in the slot with a feeling of confidence and trust. After the e-mail or letter is on its way, pause again and turn your attention inside. Offer your gratitude in spirit. What's done is done. This turns an ordinary moment into full awareness and a state of mindful grace.

You can certainly apply this lesson to what you write in blogs and on other Internet sites, as well.

148. Practice Loving-Kindness

Loving-kindness means "tender kindness motivated by or expressing affection". Here's a loving-kindness practice: "May I be free from danger. May I have mental happiness. May I have physical happiness. May I have ease of well-being." After offering these wishes to yourself, go on and wish them for others, and then the universe.

It's important to make your wishes or aspirations one after another and let them sink deep into your mind, creating far-reaching effects. Don't just recite the words in your mind, but sincerely make the wish or aspiration, understanding fully the meaning or idea behind the words.

At the beginning, the flow is not smooth and does not last long. You have to guard against merely reciting the aspiration without feeling. You also have to guard against indiscriminate and uncontrolled thinking while trying to arouse loving-kindness, which leads to restlessness. And, finally, give yourself a break if loving-kindness does not arise. This is a practice and it takes time.

Take loving-kindness breaks during the day. When you are with someone whom you find problematic, see if you can offer loving-kindness to him or her silently while you are in his or her presence. Try to incorporate the intention of loving-kindness into your listening. Listen with your heart and mind, not just your ears.

149. Free Yourself from a Bad Memory or Person

Thinking about someone else negatively or about a bad memory pollutes your inner world. Unfortunately, sometimes in this life, we are exposed to bad people or harmful events that create painful memories. If someone has seriously harmed or abused you and should no longer be in your life, even as a memory, you can use your imagination to free yourself. No matter who the person is or what the abuse was, you need to free yourself. It is not easy because you are dealing with strong and deep emotions.

Imagine putting that person or memory on a small boat and then sending the boat safely out into the ocean of life. Turn that person or memory over to the universe. You have no need to wish the person harm or good. He or she is no longer your concern. You are letting go and freeing yourself from those ties.

You are here to attain freedom from yourself, which means, simply, freedom from your memory track. Wisdom is the ability to move to your center to momentarily neutralize all of the emotional inputs and habits. The memory track is the law of karma, your cellular memory, the pattern of your existence. What you are trying to do is overcome the pattern and not listen to it. The impulse may be there, but you don't have to listen to it. You can free yourself from your memory track.

But first, you must want to be free, and you must be willing to pay a price. The price is minimal. It's called *detachment*. Why hold on to the bad person? Why hold on to the ugly experience? Let go. You must want to be free from yourself. That's the only person imprisoning you.

150. Work on Timing

Timing takes work. Whether it is a child, partner, friend, parent, boss, or coworker, you need to study his or her patterns and rhythms when it comes to talking and listening. You need to seize opportunities to talk or listen to people. Many parents value car rides for the time it allows them to talk with their children. Some couples need time alone to talk productively; others do best if they talk at a crowded restaurant.

Timing also takes understanding. Trying to force someone to talk or listen never works. When the timing is wrong, it adds stress and does not resolve problems. Trying to get people to apologize or be sorry never works, either. They're either sorry or they're not; you cannot control that.

Timing requires you to be in the right frame of mind. Talk to people as if they are doors, not walls. If you look at them as a door, they will listen and be ready to absorb what you say. If you look at them as a wall, then there will be no way to communicate effectively with them.

Make sure your timing is appropriate. If a matter is urgent, don't be afraid to convey that to the person, and ask to schedule a time to talk right away.

The next time you have the urge to interrupt someone in a conversation, pause. Instead, really listen to the complete thought(s) expressed. Don't just wait for the person to finish talking so you can interject. Listen.

151. Make Eye Contact

Often our minds can be far away from our bodies. We can rush around mentally as well as physically. We sometimes feel too busy, or don't feel comfortable looking people in the eye, even with our loved ones. We send an unhappy signal when we fail to make eye contact.

It only takes seconds to pause and connect. Make it a habit to look at the people you talk to, or the people who are talking to you. Make eye contact when you say hello or good-bye.

To train yourself, concentrate on one eye of the other person. It may help to give preference to the left eye, because the left side of the brain is said to deal with emotions. Avoid staring; just look directly at the person in a relaxed manner. Remind yourself that you are hoping to have a pleasant conversation with this person—there's no need to be anxious. Use your ears! Focus completely on what that person is saying and you won't have to worry, "Am I making eye contact correctly?" If you are truly listening, you will just naturally focus your eyes on the person's eyes.

We can give a lot to other people through simple glances. We can let them know they are loved or understood or respected without a single word being spoken.

152. Know What Children Need

Anyone who has children can attest to the pressures felt when raising children. Children need you to be a parent, not a buddy, friend, coach, or therapist. That's not what they need from you. They need you to be the grown-up so they can be the child. They need the safety of boundaries and values.

They need you to be aware of the consequences of what you do, to stand back from some of your emotions and deal with theirs with equanimity, however raw. They need you to be able to meet their needs. They need to learn that how they treat other people will dramatically affect the quality of their lives.

Children need you to show them sufficient respect so that they can make their own mistakes, and, eventually, their own decisions. They need both space and support to discover their strengths and values.

Parenting is not optional. It's not what you do when you feel like it, and children are not just things to fill empty moments in your life, only to be dropped when something or someone more interesting comes along. Children deserve a parent's loyalty, good humor, curiosity and interest, delight, infinite time and patience, and love.

153. Know What Makes You Happy

Take a quiet moment alone and try to figure out what really makes you happy. Be honest and true to your feelings. Is your happiness derived mainly from outer circumstances, things, events? How much of your happiness is due to your state of mind and the way you experience the world?

If happiness comes from outer circumstances, check how stable or fragile they are. If it is due to a state of mind, consider how you can further cultivate it. Happiness comes not from reaching out but from letting go and opening to what is true in the moment.

The Web site www.authentichappiness.org is based on the work of Dr. Martin Seligman, author of *Authentic Happiness*. The site features a questionnaire that helps you identify your key character strengths. The questionnaire takes about fifteen to twenty minutes to complete, and consists of a series of statements, like "I am never too busy to help a friend." You mark whether it is "very much like me," "very much unlike me," or somewhere in between. At the end you are given five "signature strengths" that give you insight into what really makes you happy.

Remember, too, that the more you are concerned about the happiness of others, the more you are building your own happiness at the same time. Do not expect anything in return. Think only of what is good for the other person, and you will increase your own happiness, as well.

154. Develop Your Attention

The quality of attention helps you notice all the little things in life, the little things that give you happiness. This exercise helps you develop attention and become more aware of the benefits of being attentive.

Sit quietly in a posture that feels most comfortable to you, with your back straight as if you are being pulled up by a string, and focus all of your attention upon a chosen object. It can be an object in the room, your breath, or your mind. Inevitably as you do this, your mind will wander. Each time it does, gently bring it back to the object of concentration—like a butterfly to a flower for feeding.

As you persevere, your concentration will become more clear and stable. If you start to feel sleepy, assume a straighter posture and lift your gaze slightly upward to revive your awareness. If your mind becomes agitated or distracted, relax your posture and direct your gaze slightly downward, to let your inner tension dissolve. Feel yourself gain control of your attention. Start by doing this activity for five minutes. Then try to increase it by five minutes, until you get to twenty or thirty minutes.

Cultivating attention and mindfulness in this way is a precious tool. Doing anything we love to do with mindful awareness can be an effective meditation. Meditation is not the activity, but the quality of attention that we bring to the activity.

155. Visualize

Visualization plays an important role in our memory and thinking. When we visualize, the images are like pictures in our mind. Whether we visualize from our own experience or just imagine what something is like, the actual visualization seems real to us. It helps us understand and put the world in order. We have the ability to control what we visualize. The better we can control this, the more aware we become of ourselves. By using visualization or mental imagery, we can transport ourselves to a place of peace. Here are three visualization exercises:

1. Remain calm and reasonable. Imagine another version of yourself who is egotistically self-centered. Also imagine a group of poor people unrelated to you, who are needy and suffering. Be calm and unbiased as you observe these two. Be aware that both want happiness, both want to be rid of suffering, and both have the right to accomplish these goals. Consider that we often work long and hard, willing to make temporary sacrifices for a long-term goal. By the same logic, one person could make sacrifices in order to help a larger good. This would benefit a greater number of people. The point is that you must serve and help other beings.

2. Imagine yourself and your body as a clear ball of light—crystal clear, luminous, a sphere of white light, a pure being. Envision a golden sun at the heart center, opening like a sunflower. Warm and illumine all who wander through the darkness of ignorance and delusion. Awaken spiritual awareness and joy like the dawn. Let go and see the afterglow. Simply be in the joy and peace of this meditation.

3. Practice confidence visualization for difficult situations: Relax the tension from your body, breathe three deep breaths, and then breathe naturally. Visualize yourself entering into the challenging situation with confidence. See yourself exuding self-confidence. Keep this image in your mind for as long as possible. Reinforce the visualization by repeating an affirmation, like "I can handle this" or "I am very confident."

156. Exchange Happiness and Suffering

As we gain more knowledge and grow spiritually, we begin to look at the world in a different light. We begin to realize that we have a tremendous amount of control over how we feel and how we perceive the world. We can use this power to exchange happiness and suffering. By generating a powerful feeling of warmth, loving-kindness, and compassion for all beings, you can train yourself in the exchange of happiness and suffering. This can be done anywhere and anytime. You don't need any tools or devices, just the right frame of mind. By first admitting that you want well-being, you take the first step toward feeling genuine empathy for others. It allows you to adjust your reaction to unavoidable suffering by changing its value.

Imagine those who are suffering in ways similar to your own suffering, or worse. As you breathe out, visualize that you are sending them all of your happiness, health, and good fortune. Picture them absorbing this, which soothes their pain. If they are sick, imagine they are healed. If they are unhappy, imagine they are filled with joy. If they are hurt, imagine them healthy. If they are crying, imagine them laughing. If they are confused, imagine them steady. If they are weak, imagine them strong.

When you inhale, visualize your heart as a bright luminous sphere filled with love and hope. Imagine that you are taking in the others' suffering in the form of a gray cloud. Then imagine the gray cloud disappearing into the white light of your heart. This will transform and dissolve both your suffering and that of others. When you are doing this, feel a great happiness, without attachment or clinging to any particular outcome. You are happy in the moment.

157. Practice Insight Meditation

Insight meditation is one of the best ways to gain greater peace and happiness in your life and in the world. It helps you cultivate compassion and awareness by opening your ability to see clearly into the nature of the mind. It allows you to become acquainted with the mind and reflect on it. Through introspection and self-observation, you can transform yourself.

Sit comfortably with your eyes closed and resolve for five minutes to observe only the thought process. For these five minutes, count each thought as it arises. Your thoughts may come as picture thoughts or as words, or both together. Some thoughts may also come associated with a feeling or bodily sensation.

Let your mind be blank like a clear screen or open space, and wait to count each thought, like a cat waiting by a mouse hole. After noticing and counting a thought, just wait for the next one. Do not let yourself be fooled by the thoughts. Some of them are very quiet, like "It's quiet in here," and some appear from behind, like "There haven't been a lot of thoughts yet." These are thoughts and need to be counted, too.

At the end of five minutes, most people will have seen at least five to ten thoughts and many will have counted fifty to sixty. You will see what types of thoughts predominate in your mind—words or pictures, etc.—and their content, like "planning" or "ruminating."

You will get a sense of how well you observe your thought process with mindfulness, noticing the arising of thought without getting lost in its story. It is a powerful and freeing realization to see that you are not your thoughts, to observe the stream of consciousness of inner thought, and to be aware of it without being identified and caught up in it.

158. Calm the Mind

Our minds are often racing. We have so much on our plate that we feel overwhelmed, causing us to think too much. When this happens to us, we need to calm our minds to put things in proper perspective. Here is an exercise for calming the mind and looking within.

Sit in a comfortable position, body erect but not tense, with the eyes gently open. For five minutes, breathe calmly, noticing the in-and-out of the breath. Experience the gradual calming of chaotic thoughts. When the thoughts arise, do not attempt to block them or shoo them away or let them multiply. Simply continue to watch the breath.

Instead of paying attention to outer sights, sounds, and happenings, turn your "gaze" inward and look at the mind itself. Looking means observing your actual awareness, not the content of your thoughts. Let the mind gently come to rest, like a weary traveler.

With a deep feeling of appreciation, think of the value of human existence and of its potential for flourishing. Be aware, too, that your own precious human life will not last forever, and it is essential to make the best of it. Sincerely examine what is of value to you, what your priorities are in life. What do you need to accomplish or to discard in order to achieve well-being, happiness, and a meaningful existence? When the factors that contribute to true happiness have become clear to you, imagine that they bloom like a flower in your mind. Resolve to nurture this flower every day.

End this exercise by letting thoughts of pure kindness embrace you and all living beings. Appreciate your calm mind.

159. Experience Optimism and Pessimism

We cannot feel optimistic if from time to time we do not feel pessimistic. You can experience both feelings, yet in the end, be in control and appreciate the optimistic state. The following is an experiment in how to view the same situation through the eyes of both optimism and pessimism.

Let's say you are on a long car ride with your family to a vacation spot. You suddenly encounter a lot of traffic you were not anticipating. You are uncomfortable in your seat and your mind is filled with complaints about the trip. You are annoyed with the children, who are either jabbering or making irritating noises with their video games. When you think ahead to the vacation itself, you dread the idea of all of you staying in the same room and the children wanting to watch television instead of wanting to go sightseeing or doing physical activities. You worry about whether the room will be nice and how you will all share one bathroom. You worry about whether the children will behave at meals. You start thinking that the trip will be a disaster. How did you ever come up with this idea? You are filled with dread. Experience the state of mind these thoughts create.

Then experiment with another way to look at the same situation. When the traffic thickens, you know that it is part of the journey, and feel that every moment you have here with your family is precious. As the traffic lightens up, you feel grateful and hope that you can use the rest of this trip constructively. Although your seat is not particularly comfortable, you find positions to relieve stiffness. You appreciate that your partner talks to you pleasantly during the ride. You imagine that your vacation destination will be interesting and that you will have many opportunities for fun with your family. You are convinced that the stay will be a good experience and you will have many fond memories of the trip. Try to create some laughter in the car to get the energy flowing. Experience the buoyant state of mind that comes from these thoughts.

Appreciate the difference between these two states of mind and understand how they came about simply through the workings of your mind, even though the external circumstances and situation remained the same. Appreciate that you are able to control these feelings.

160. *Practice Walking Meditation*

You can use walking meditation to calm and collect yourself and to live more mindfully in your body. You can extend your walking practice to when you go shopping, whenever you walk down the street, or to and from your car. This practice allows you to enjoy walking for its own sake instead of filling it up with the usual planning and thinking.

- *Begin with your feet firmly planted on the ground. Let your arms and hands rest easily.*
- *Close your eyes for a moment, centering yourself and taking a few deep breaths.*
- *Feel yourself standing on the earth. Feel the pressure of the bottoms of your feet on the ground. Feel the sensations of standing.*
- *Then open your eyes and be present and aware.*
- *Begin to walk slowly. Walk with ease and dignity.*
- *With each step feel all of the sensations involved in lifting your foot and leg up from the earth.*
- *Be aware as you place each foot back onto the earth.*
- *Relax and let your walking be easy and natural. Be mindful of each step.*

- *Your mind will wander many times, just as it does when you're sitting.*
- *As soon as you notice this, acknowledge it, and then return to feel the next step.*

Whether your mind has wandered for one second or ten minutes, simply acknowledge this and come back to being aware of the next step you take. At the midpoint of your walk, pause for a moment. Center yourself and carefully turn around. Pause again so you can be aware of the first step as you walk back. Walk simply, being truly present. At the end of the path, please pause. Try to carry the momentum of your mindfulness into whatever your next activity may be.

161. Practice "Open Presence"

Here is a form of meditation where the mind is not focused on any particular thing and yet it is not distracted by anything, either. Thoughts vanish naturally instead of you trying to banish them. It can be described as entering into the flow of "open presence."

Sit in a comfortable meditation position, eyes gently open, posture straight. Quiet your mind. Try to make your mind as vast and open as the sky. Do not focus on anything. Remain relaxed, calm, fully aware.

Let your mind remain free from mental constructs, clear and vivid, effortless and undistracted. Without actively trying to block sense perceptions, imagination, recollections, and ruminations, feel that you are uninfluenced and unmoved by them as they arise. Remain at ease.

Do not allow perceptions to alter the vastness and serenity of your mind. Whenever thoughts arise, let them undo themselves as they form, like ripples on the surface of a lake that appear and then smooth out. Acknowledge emotions for what they are, and allow them to pass through you like wind through the leaves of a tree. Let them be without judging or getting caught up in them.

Experience the peace you feel for as long as possible after this exercise.

162. Do Projects

Even on a sunny day, the world might look cloudy to you. When you feel this, take a proactive philosophy to help yourself. Turn off the television, stop moaning and crabbing to whoever is on the other end of the phone, and make sure you get your behind out of bed before noon. Instead of being slothful and hanging a poor me sign on your back, get busy on some projects!

Why? Because working on projects is an excellent way to prop yourself up when you are not feeling so good about where you're at in your life. You simply cannot underestimate the power of a sense of accomplishment. You may not be close to finishing that 500-page novel you've been writing, but you can certainly complete some sort of cool project—and once you put the finishing touches on a smaller project, you'll feel like you can get that novel done in no time.

Take this effort one step further and create projects with other people in mind, to give to them as gifts. You get the satisfaction of completing projects and also making others smile. Acts of kindness go a long way. Knowing that you have brought some happiness to others is going to give you a wonderful feeling of satisfaction. You will feel like the world is not such a bad place, and you can move forward from whatever has been dragging you down. Suddenly, you feel ready to take on whatever life throws at you.

163. Read More Books

Reading a great book can affect you in a positive way. Part of your journey toward more happiness is reflecting on how you were shaped. It is good to take the time to make a list of books that have changed your life. Explore how reading has helped shape your life, your work, your relationships. Think of the books that you feel people miss out on if they do not read them, the books you felt like you were "watching" as you read them. We should respect the power of reading to shape our lives and world.

To think about this, go back to the books you checked out of the library as a kid, the books stored at your parents' house, the ones in your attic. Wander around a bookstore to stir some memories. After just a little thought, you will be able to recall many titles that changed your life.

Reading is a way to live more lives, to experience more worlds, to meet people you care about and want to know more about, and, especially, to understand others and develop a compassion for what they confront and endure. You celebrate what you have read in your life by making this list. To that end, here's my list: *Little Women, Walden, A Horse and His Boy, Seeking the Heart of Wisdom,*

Encyclopaedia Britannica, The Power of Kindness, The Art of the Moment, Grace Notes, Astonish Yourself!, Into the Wild.

Go to the library or bookstore and seek out other books written by the same authors on your list.

164. Write Down Your Favorite Quotes

Quotations can be great reminders or "prompts" to snap us back to reality, and to remind us to be grateful and appreciate the little things. What about happiness quotes? Do you use these to cheer yourself?

Write down all of your favorite quotes—the ones on or under the magnets stuck to your refrigerator, featured on the greeting cards you buy to mail to friends, or written in your journal. Look at quote books or online references. After you have written down your list of quotes, take a few minutes to analyze them. Why do these quotes impact you? Why have they become personal anthems? What larger body of work do they come from, and have you read any of these? Do your favorite quotes come from a certain time frame? Do the quotes teach lessons? Can a family member, friend, or coworker benefit from your quotes? Appreciate the power of your quotes. This can be an ongoing exercise for you; whenever you read a great quote, write it down and keep it.

165. Wake Up Before Everyone

Wake up really early, for yourself. Do it just to take advantage of the quiet early-morning hours. You can meditate, walk, go for a run, do yoga. You can leisurely read a newspaper. You can write in your journal or work on your novel. How about making a huge breakfast? Or you can just sit, drink your coffee, and watch the sun rise. If you decide to wake up an hour earlier than you normally do, this time can be used for your personal projects. Being productive from the moment you roll out of bed is a great way to start your day.

Make a list of the stuff you always *have* to get done and how long it takes you to do it all. Document your time for everything, not just your work. How long does all this stuff really take? How much time do you spend spinning your wheels, getting organized, worrying about getting things done?

Then, write down everything you *want* to do—all the things you feel you never have enough time to actually dive into. Once it is all written down, spend some time thinking about how you can use the early-morning hours to accomplish some of these things, to strike a better balance between the items on both lists. Be sure to make the things you *want* to do a part of what *has* to get done.

166. Annotate Your Books

Write in the margins of your books. Annotate your books with comments and opinions. Underline your favorite passages and quotations. Underline things that make you happy. Underline good ideas.

Once you highlight, underline, or annotate your books, you can choose to transfer the information to a journal. You can begin a journal of knowledge or interesting things from your new routine. Be creative with the process. Another great thing to do after you have written down information from a book is to donate or sell the book and put them back into circulation. It will be funny to think how you are influencing others by the highlights, underlines, or notes you put into the book.

Everyone should just plain get over the taboo of writing in their own books. Make notes about the content, things the content reminds you of, etc. There are plenty of other ways to take this further (i.e., Post-it notes can be used to mark interesting passages). Your books will feel more personal if you give yourself permission to remove the dust jacket, dog-ear or Post-it some pages, underline passages, and write in the margins.

167. Read Your Writings

Find the first poem you ever wrote, the first journal, maybe even the first letter you wrote or received. After reading one of these, try to remember the story of why you wrote it, what inspired you, and who it was for. Write all this down and then write a new poem, a new letter, a new journal entry. You can expand this to other writings, like the first story you ever wrote.

If you have the first journal or diary, or any journal of yours from an earlier time, this makes for interesting reading. Sit down and read it, making notes in your current journal. What can you remember like it was yesterday? What significant events do you have no recall of? What makes you feel embarrassed or proud? What lessons have you learned?

Photographs and artwork can be used, too. Find the first pictures you took or your artwork from elementary school. What do these early works tell you about yourself? Go through old photos or pictures until you get to one that evokes an unexpected response.

Go through old photographs of family and friends and find one connected to an important story. Write a story about that event and how your feelings and recall of it have changed over time.

168. Pick a Cheerful Place to Go

The next time you are feeling down or depressed, instead of just sitting there watching mind-numbing television, get outta there if at all possible. Go to a place that cheers you up. The place should either have good memories for you or be a place where you can just feel safe and comfortable. Pick a place that feels alive to you or has a lot of positive energy.

Some people feel better escaping to a movie, to stop their mind from thinking. Not a bad idea, but the movie must be uplifting or funny! When you leave the movie, you should find yourself in a happier mood.

Don't go to a place where you will feel more alone in the world. Sitting in a park or coffee shop or library alone may make some people ruminate and think even more and then feel worse. If you can put yourself in a place filled with activity, that's great. Also, shopping when you are down or depressed is a big mistake; you'll end up buying something you don't need and then you'll feel badly about doing it.

169. Wait While Doing Nothing

This is a calming exercise to use in a doctor's or dentist's waiting room, a government office, an airport or train station—places you have to wait, where there might be a delay. You know that eventually you will be called into the office, the train or plane will arrive and then leave. The outcome is certain. You are forced to be passive, though, as there is nothing you can do to speed up the process. You are confronted with the unavoidable passage of time, passing more or less slowly.

A lot of people find this type of situation very difficult to put up with. They contrive to avoid this head-on encounter with time by reading magazines, novels, essays, taking notes, using a BlackBerry or cell phone, listening to an iPod, or working on a laptop. In short, they keep busy, filling the given span of time with activities, big or little ideas, and a variety of tasks.

This experiment is exactly the reverse. Do nothing. Without becoming irritated or bored, do nothing. Let yourself float in time, knowing that it will pass, inexorably, in you and outside of you. You need to merge without anxiety into this total passivity.

Everything will happen and nothing depends on you. You can be empty, indifferent, dreamy, whatever—and time moves on regardless. The waiting interval will come to an end. You can make the discovery that there is no need to kill time. It dies on its own, unceasingly.

170. Try Not to Think

This experiment will show you that trying *not* to think is one of the most difficult (or nearly impossible) activities you will ever try. Not to think at all, when one is wide awake and in possession of one's faculties, cannot be achieved—or if it can, only for short intervals. But it can be attempted.

Why is not thinking impossible? The experience of it would remove you from the sphere of the human, allow you to escape the incessant babble of language, put you into a pure moment-to-moment animal life. You would fall into a divine, abyssal silence. Thinking may be the in-between, between silence and words, presence and absence, being and non-being.

Thinking cannot be stopped definitively. You can interrupt it, especially if you are a regular meditator. It is no help to think that you are not thinking. It is better to know in advance how hard this is, and that you will catch yourself thinking during the experiment. Here are the steps to follow: Sit and let your thoughts flow by. Don't stop them, but also, don't hold on to them. Observe them as you do passing clouds, far off and inevitable. Be indifferent, like the sky. Persevere in remaining unclouded and paying no attention to what is passing by. That is all. See thoughts and sensations, but do not judge or hold them. Occasionally you will feel like you are becoming more like the clear sky. Every momentary success will have a lasting effect.

171. Browse through Books

The energy inside a bookstore is powerful. All the knowledge, all the stories, all the art is just there, waiting to be absorbed and enjoyed.

Take a few hours to go to a giant bookstore or several smaller bookstores, especially secondhand/used bookstores. You are entering into the entire range of book titles.

You go from shelf to shelf, stack to stack, wall to wall. You are not looking for anything in particular. You will feel certain titles, authors, characters calling you, trying to get your attention. The competition is intense. Among these thousands of books, which voices will you choose to follow? Each book wants you to notice it. Each lives a little longer because of the attention it gets. Even when you end this experiment, you will hear them calling out to you. Feel compassion for those authors who spent so much time writing these books, pouring it all out on paper for you.

What did you learn about yourself during this browsing adventure?

172. Become Music

Music is one of those powerful influences in our lives. Remember some of the songs that have affected you over the years. Whether jazz, rock, classical, or any other kind, few things can impact us like music. This experiment will let you see music like you have never seen it before. It will help you *be* the music. Put on some music you really like, turn up the volume full blast, and close your eyes. Relax every muscle, stretch out, dissolve. Nothing but the music. Wait—and let go.

Make no effort. Just be the music. Dissolve into its notes, rhythms, and timbres. You will feel wordless and float in the sound. Nothing remains but sound waves.

The experiment is to now see yourself as the music. You are simply present in the music.

173. Walk in a Forest of Imagination

This is a different type of meditation that requires lots of visualization. Find a forest to walk in, one where you can walk briskly and for a fairly long time. You walk without attending to anything except the synchrony of regular breathing and walking.

You have to work up a tempo of walking where if you stop, the trees keep moving. Imagine that the forest is your soul and you are walking like this within yourself. You are strolling through the inside of your own mind and thoughts. See what is there, like you would see trees and brush as you walk in the forest. But don't dwell on anything you see.

You start to realize that the mind has nothing outside itself, or if it has, then you can choose to know nothing about it.

174. Watch Someone Sleeping

You can watch someone you know very well while he or she sleeps. It is not as weird as it first sounds. This is a person you know every inch of—his or her voice, beliefs, personality—both physical and mental characteristics. But when you watch the person, you will probably get the impression that you don't know him or her completely.

The face is different with the eyes closed. The body is different as it lies there. The breathing sounds far away, and the posture is unusual. You have no idea what he or she is dreaming about. It may seem like a scene you should not be witnessing. But relax. It is okay to watch.

The juxtaposition of presence and absence creates this unease. The sleeping person seems very different from the awake person. You are seeing the person in an unfamiliar light. It is important to get beyond this feeling and focus on the calm that the person is experiencing while sleeping.

Watching people sleep is calming, too, because someone in the world is experiencing a sense of calm, even if it's not you. The human in repose at close quarters is known but unknown. You are aware of the grandeur of the mind when someone sleeps—the body still, motivations temporarily suspended—so what's left is the vast interior space. Dreaming or not, neurons fire off echoes of earlier experience, repeating and learning and storing up impressions for use in waking life. It's all in there, rattling around the endless architecture of memory in this person's mind. We are always at close proximity to one another, and only our adherence to resistance and denial keeps this kind of intimacy at bay.

175. Smile at Strangers

Have you ever had a stranger smile at you? Your eyes meet and the person smiles at you. If it is truly just a smile, with no strings attached, the experience probably made a positive impression on you.

On the street, in shops, at work, at the grocery store, in town, abroad or in your own country, you encounter many people you don't know. You have never seen them before and will never see them again, especially in a large city, at a tourist attraction, or overseas. You may have no desire to communicate anything to these strangers.

Try smiling. Smile in a discreet, restrained, clear, reserved (but benevolent) way. When your eyes meet a stranger's, just smile. The smile shows tolerance and acceptance, and says, "You are in the world with me."

Hopefully, this experiment will soften you and create good karma. So, smile at strangers more. Sometimes you will get a real smile, a truly happy one in return. Other times, people will not react at all. Don't worry about that; it's not personal. They are just not used to getting smiles from strangers.

A simple act of kindness such as a smile can end up meaning so much more . . . maybe even saving a life. Have fun with this one.

176. Enter a Painting

The next time you are at a museum or looking through an art book, I want you to try this experiment: Take a deep breath and relax and fall into the painting or drawing you are looking at. It may seem silly at first, but give it a chance. Have some fun with your imagination. Think of Alice falling down the rabbit hole if it helps. You might get lucky and fall into a painting!

Stop at the paintings or drawings that attract you. If you are at a museum, you can sit on a bench in front of the painting or drawing. If you are looking at a book, find a comfortable chair to sit in. Picture yourself falling in and becoming part of the painting. Let the painting seize you and allow yourself to get carried away. Take in the painting or picture and feel the atmosphere of the art. Become part of the time period pictured in the artwork. Enjoy your journey; it's taking you someplace, so enjoy it. Art can be an intense experience.

At a glance you can take in the picture and also the feeling and atmosphere. For some, this is better than reading words.

177. Play with a Child

Find a very young child, preferably one who cannot yet talk or who talks very little (under three years old). Choose a game that he or she knows well and has mastered, and go along with it. Your role is simply to follow and join in, in his or her way, not yours. You are in his or her world now.

Accept the endless repetitions, crazy rules, delays, and inexplicable moments of merriment. Observe the concentration that is taking place with the child. Recognize that he or she is totally in the present moment. The child's whole world consists only of what he or she is doing right now. In this experiment, you enter this world of the child's game and leave your normal adult universe behind.

The goal is to become part of the child's game. You should not be a passive observer here, but instead, become a true participant in the child's world. Don't think about what time it is or all the things you feel you need to do. You want your world to meld with the child's world.

Afterward, explore the effects of this play once you've returned to the normal world. This is the heart of the experiment. If you have left behind the thread of your own thoughts, completely enough and for long enough, there is a chance that you won't be able to pick right up where you left off in the adult world. You will feel bewildered and find yourself groping for your bearings. This is normal and healthy. It is good to question how you feel in the adult world.

Entering the world of the child's game has "de-structured" you, and now you have to work to recover yourself. You are disorganized inside. You have to work to put things back in their places. You may want to meditate on this new territory that you consider to be your "normal" mental state.

178. Create a Happiness Map of What You Want Life to Look Like

Through this exercise, you can discover the potential of your associative machinery, as well as some insight into your individuality. Fill in quickly, with single key words printed on the lines, and without pausing to choose, the first ten associations that radiate from the center when you think of the concept of *happiness*. It is important to put down the first words that come into your mind, no matter how ridiculous they may seem. This should take about a minute total.

Now look at the map you've created. Based on the data you collected, envision your ideal week. If you want to spend more time reading and less time watching TV, write down the amount of time that you think is ideal for each. Be realistic. Then put it into practice. If you have many constraints and cannot introduce significant change, make the most of what you do have. Consider what kinds of brief activities—ones that provide you with both present and future benefit—you could introduce into your life.

From this one word and one exercise, you can see that any word or sensation is a tiny center with potentially thousands or millions of associations emanating from it. When you complete this exercise with others, you can also see that the associations you wrote down are magically different from those of another person. Look at the associations you made to the word *happiness*. What do they say about you? What are the obvious patterns? Do you have control over many of the associations, or do you feel that they are out of your control?

It's important to repeat this exercise periodically, because your life, mood, and awareness constantly change over time. What you map out on one day may be quite different from what you map out on another day, a month (or a year) later.

179. Perform The Meaning, Pleasure, and Strengths Process

The Meaning, Pleasure, and Strengths Process is an exercise that helps you understand aspects of yourself so that you can lead a happier life. You do not have to be in a crisis to complete this exercise. It is helpful to do throughout your life. It begins by asking three crucial questions:

1. What gives me meaning?

2. What gives me pleasure?

3. What are my strengths?

After you answer the above questions, continue by noting and analyzing the trends that emerge. In your analysis, look at the answers and identify areas of overlap. This will help you determine what kind of work and play make you happiest.

Generating accurate answers to these questions requires more effort than simply jotting down whatever comes to mind. Most of us have more or less ready-made answers to such questions. While the answers may be true, they probably stop short of representing the full range of experiences that answer the questions. We want to gain the added benefit of taking our answers a bit further, so, please, spend time reflecting and thinking deeply.

Whether the lists generated from answering the questions are short or long does not matter. The important aspect of this exercise is to see the overlap of the answers. Once you discover that, you will be able to seek out things that give you more meaning and pleasure while utilizing your strengths—which will ultimately lead you to more happiness and success.

180. Meditate on Benevolence

Meditation can come in many forms. During this meditation, think back to a time when you behaved benevolently toward someone else and felt appreciated for it. In your mind's eye, see the person's response to your act. Savor it.

Experience your own feelings and allow them to materialize inside you. As you see the other person and experience your own feelings, break the artificial divide that exists between helping yourself and helping others. This is a fine line. Most people believe that helping others is like helping yourself.

Now think of a future opportunity. Think of more ways you can be benevolent toward others. It could be sharing an idea, giving flowers, reading to someone, donating to a cause. Experience the deep happiness that can come with each act of generosity. Feel the world becoming a better place.

181. Meditate on Happiness

Try to find some happiness in each day, no matter what happens. One of the best ways to achieve this goal is to meditate on happiness. By experiencing more happiness in your life, you will have a positive impact on yourself, as well as others. Find a quiet spot and sit in your meditation position. You can close your eyes or keep them open. Enter a state of calm by breathing three deep breaths and then breathe normally. Relax and follow the breath for five minutes. If your mind wanders, gently bring it back to your breathing.

Now focus on a positive emotion. You may imagine yourself when you were particularly happy. For a few minutes, reexperience the positive emotions and allow them to rise inside you. If you do this meditation regularly, you will attain the capacity to bring up positive emotions just by thinking of the word *happiness*, *calm*, or *joy*.

Set aside time for this practice on a regular basis, even if it is done while riding in a car or on a train, waiting somewhere, or at your desk.

182. Count Your Breath

Breathing is probably the most natural thing we do in life. It is one of the main functions to sustain life. However, most of the time we are not mindful or conscious of our breathing. Our breathing reflects our emotions. When we are stressed, our breathing becomes rapid. If you learn how to count your breaths, then you can make your breathing calm and even.

As you breathe in, count 1 in your mind, and as you breathe out, count 1. Breathe in, count 2. Breathe out, count 2. Continue through 10, then return again to 1.

This counting is like a string that attaches mindfulness to your breath. The exercise is the starting point of the process of becoming continuously conscious of your breath. Without mindfulness, though, you will quickly lose count. When you lose count, simply return to 1 and keep trying until you can reach 10.

Once you can focus your attention on the count up to 10, you have reached the point at which you can begin to abandon the counting method and concentrate solely on the breath.

At times when you are upset or discombobulated and find it difficult to practice mindfulness, return to your breath. Taking hold of your breath is, in and of itself, practicing mindfulness. Learn to practice breathing in these ways in order to regain control of body and mind, to practice mindfulness, and develop concentration and wisdom.

183. Have a Day of Mindfulness

A day of mindfulness is like a mini retreat for yourself. In our busy lives, a day of mindfulness can be a difficult thing to work in. But try to reserve one day of each week, month, quarter, or year to devote to the practice of mindfulness. As you practice this exercise more and more, you will be surprised at how you begin to find more time to do it.

Whatever day you choose, it must be entirely *your* day. From the very moment you wake up, you realize that today is your day. While you are still lying in bed, follow your breath as it rises, pauses, and falls.

Once up, brush your teeth, wash your face, and do all of your morning activities in a calm and relaxing way, each movement done in mindfulness. Follow your breathing, taking long, quiet breaths. Maintain a half-smile throughout.

Spend at least a half-hour taking a bath. Do this mindfully and slowly so that when you finish, you feel light and refreshed. Afterward, you may attend to some light household duties, but do them slowly, with ease and mindfulness. Enjoy and be one with each task. It is best to maintain a spirit of silence. If you do talk, keep it to a minimum, and do it with complete mindfulness. This is difficult in a family setting, but ask your family to respect your wishes and try to help you out.

When you prepare your meals, cook, eat, and do dishes with mindfulness. If you have a cup of tea or coffee, do this slowly and reverently. Be in the actual moment. Do not think about the next thing. And every movement during this day should be at least two times slower than usual.

In the evening, you might read or do something outside like take a walk, but again, always in mindfulness. You can intersperse meditation of five to twenty minutes between activities, and especially just before bed. Then do a relaxation exercise for five to ten minutes. Prepare for bed with mindfulness, and go to sleep with a sense of peace.

184. Half-Smile

Put a sign or Post-it note on the ceiling or wall that says SMILE so that you see it right away when you wake up in the morning. This will serve as your reminder. Use the second before you get out of bed to inhale and exhale three deep breaths while maintaining a half-smile. Follow the breaths.

Anywhere you go and whatever you do, keep a half-smile on your face. Look at something that is still and smile. When you listen to music, smile. Wherever you sit or stand, smile. Maintain the half-smile and be attentive.

When you realize you are irritated, half-smile at once. Inhale and exhale quietly, maintaining the half-smile for at least three breaths.

When you see someone smile, you know immediately that he or she is dwelling in awareness. This half-smile . . . how many artists have labored to bring it to the lips of countless statues and paintings? Mona Lisa's smile is light, just a hint of a smile. Yet even a smile like that is enough to relax all the muscles in your face, to banish all worries and fatigue. A tiny bud of a smile on your lips nourishes awareness and calms you miraculously, returning you to peace.

185. Do a Relaxation Pose

The relaxation pose is a yoga position that will benefit you either when you first wake up in the morning, or when used as a refresher sometime during the day. It does not matter what time of the day it is, performing the relaxation pose will help you. When you are in the relaxation pose, your heart and pulse rate will quiet and you will develop body and mind awareness. It is a difficult pose to master because it requires you to let go of everything and relax. This is very hard for us to do. Below is a basic set of instructions.

- *Find a comfortable place to lie down on your back, but not so comfortable that you will be likely to fall asleep.*
- *Your arms should lie slightly out from your sides, palms up. Your legs should be separate and fall open, relaxed. Your eyes should be closed.*
- *Sense your whole body, especially the points where it touches the surface you are lying on.*
- *Follow your breath and then bring your awareness to your feet. Wiggle your toes, flex and relax the feet, letting go of any tension there.*
- *Bring your awareness to your lower legs, slightly tensing the muscles and then relaxing them. Do this for your thighs. Then do this for your hips.*
- *Bring your awareness to your abdomen. Think of the tension draining away, your abdomen opening and softening. Continue to follow and observe your breath also.*
- *Bring your awareness to your upper abdomen and rib cage, feeling the areas open and soften. Then do this for your chest, and then your neck and throat.*

- Bring your awareness to your shoulders. Feel their heaviness melting into the surface. Do this with your upper arms, then the lower arms. Wiggle your fingers, flex, and relax them, letting go of any tension there.
- Now bring awareness to your head and face. Feel the tension and then let it melt into the surface.
- Feel the calm now in each part of your body. If when you scan your body from head to toe, you feel an area of tension, then imagine that area relaxing.
- When you have scanned your entire body, go back to the breath. You will continue this way for five to fifteen minutes, following the breath.
- Now slowly wiggle your fingers and toes. Begin to stretch your arms and legs. Open your eyes slowly. Gradually come to a sitting position. Try to carry the momentum of your mindfulness into whatever your next activity may be.

186. Develop Compassion

A great quote about compassion by Mason Cooley says a lot: "Compassion brings us to a stop, and for a moment we rise above ourselves." This signifies the importance of compassion, and why it's truly one of the greatest gifts in life.

In our lives, we meet people who cause us suffering, or we may find something about them that we just do not like. We may even feel that we hate or despise certain people. This exercise helps you develop compassion toward such people and will set you free.

Start by getting into a sitting meditation posture. Breathe and smile a half-smile. Contemplate the image of the person who has caused you the most suffering. Regard the features you hate or despise the most, or find the most repulsive.

Try to examine what makes this person happy and what causes suffering in his or her daily life. Contemplate the person's perceptions; try to see the patterns of thought and reason that this person follows. Examine what motivates this person's hopes and actions. Then consider the person's consciousness. Are his or her views open and free, or not? Are they influenced by prejudice, narrow-mindedness, hatred, or anger?

Continue until you feel compassion rise in your heart and your anger and resentment disappear. Practice this exercise regularly until you are able to let go of your hatred. You will experience true freedom when you can master this.

187. Practice Yin Yoga

Yin yoga contains the ancient, and some say original, form of yoga practice. The sages who pioneered the path of yoga used these exercises to strengthen the body so that they could sit for long periods in contemplative meditation. If you have ever sat for a long time with legs crossed, you know the hips and lower back need to be strong and open. The sensations you felt were deep in the connective tissues and the joints. These are the deep yin tissues of the body, relative to the more superficial yang tissues of muscles and skin. Yin yoga opens up these deep, dense, rarely touched areas.

There are not nearly as many asanas (yogic postures) required in the yin style of yoga as are found in the more active yoga practices. There are perhaps three dozen postures at most, a basic sixteen, and of these, half are seated positions. The yin areas of the body generally targeted in the practice are between the knees and navel, the lower body. Since the poses are held longer, there are fewer poses that one can even attempt in one session. One goes into a yin pose as deep as he or she comfortably can, resolves to remain still, and holds the pose for as long as possible. Yin yoga is something to look into whether you practice yoga regularly or not. You can go to a class, watch a video, or read a book on yin yoga that will help you get started. It addresses the deep tissues of the body that do not get stretched or worked by any other types of exercise. Acupuncture meridians are also located in connective tissues, and yin yoga is specifically designed to stimulate them.

188. Complete a Weekly Work Exercise

Depending on your circumstances in life, a week can be viewed as a short time or a long time. It all has to do with your perception of things. For this exercise, view a week as the first step of the rest of your life. Explore each of the hindrances you may face in a week's time. Notice your relationship to each one:

- *desire (for some particular experience)*
- *ill will or aversion*
- *sloth and torpor (drowsiness)*
- *restlessness*
- *doubt*

Undertake for one week to purposefully bring no harm in thought, word, or deed to any living creature. Particularly become aware of any living beings in your world whom you ignore, and cultivate a sense of care and reverence for them, too.

Undertake for one week to act on every single thought of generosity that arises spontaneously in your heart.

Undertake for one week not to gossip (positively or negatively), or to speak about anyone you know who is not present with you.

Undertake for one week to observe meticulously how often sexual feelings and thoughts arise in your consciousness. Each time, note what particular mind states are associated with them, such as aggression, caring, compulsion, desire for communication, greed, loneliness, love, pleasure, tension, etc.

Undertake for one week (or one month) to refrain from all intoxicants and addictive substances (even caffeine, if you wish). Observe the impulses to use these and become aware of what is going on in the heart and mind at the time of those impulses.

After you have done this for a week, reflect on how you feel. How are you different than you were the week before? How do you feel now? What have you learned?

189. Observe Intention

To understand karma, it is essential to see how the motivation or intention preceding an action determines the result of that action. If an act is motivated by true kindness, it will bring a positive result. If an act is motivated by aggression or greed, it will eventually bring an unpleasant result. Because karmic results do not always bear fruit immediately, it is sometimes difficult to observe this process.

Speech is one area in which karma can be seen in an easy and direct way. For this exercise, resolve to take two to three days to carefully notice the intentions that motivate your speech. Direct your attention to the state of mind that precedes talking, the motivation for your comments, responses, and observations. Try to be particularly aware of whether your speech is even subtly motivated by boredom, compassion, competitiveness, concern, fear, greed, irritation, loneliness, love, or whatever state you observe. Be aware, too, of the general mood or state of your heart and mind, and how that may be influencing your speech.

Try to observe without any judgment. Simply notice the various motivations in the mind, and the speech that flows from them. Then, after discovering which motivation is present as you speak, notice the effect of the speech. What response does it elicit? With the law of karma, we have a choice in each new moment of what response our heart and mind will bring to the situation. In discovering the power of your inner state to determine outer conditions, you will be able to follow a path that can lead to genuine happiness.

190. Deal with Teenagers

The topic of dealing with teenagers is at least a whole book in itself. It is not easy; for you or your teenagers. More changes are happening to them both mentally and physically than at any other time in their lives. The best advice in this area is, "This too shall pass"! Realize first that the toddlers/children you once knew are gone. You have budding young adults on your hands. Cherish the memories.

Realize that breaking away from you at some level is your teenager's job at this point. At the same time, your children usually return once they have gone through this passage. In whatever way possible, maintain the relationship in a way that keeps it intact for when they need you. Remember that it's their job to act like they don't need you (even though they do, desperately). Hang in there with them.

Pick your battles wisely. You don't have to fight to win on each and every issue. Remember that the relationship is always more important than being right! And make sure your behavior matches your word. Do what you say you are going to do.

Finally, encourage your children to write, either a journal or a blog or something—as a way to get feelings out and let them go. And you should follow the same advice—keep a list of things to be happy about, a journal, a blog, something to help you get through the teenage years so you can enjoy the next stage of life with your sanity intact!

191. Prepare for the Empty Nest

Just when you feel you've perfected parenting for all stages of childhood, from infancy through the teen years, you'll find yourself without an audience. How you handle your empty nest will depend on how well you prepared yourself and your children for that day. As with all stages of life, a little preparation goes a long way. It is very normal to miss and grieve. However, this time can be viewed as a new beginning. Try to look at it as an exciting time with many new adventures in front of you.

From a young age, it is important to encourage your children to be independent and do things on their own, spend time with friends, spend time away from home, and you. Set a good example by showing them that you, too, have parts of your life that are just for you. When your children leave the nest and you find yourself struggling to cope, try to think in terms of getting over it quickly, so you can help them succeed in this new phase of his or her life. Add this item to your list of responsibilities: "Have a life."

Parents, you have a responsibility to your children to take care of yourselves. Stay in close communication with your spouses, friends, and family, and make time for yourselves. You should also stick to your own independent agendas, and continue to foster your own plans and dreams. Doing this even before the children leave the nest also sets a good example for them.

Talk things over with friends, especially ones who are going through or have gone through the empty nest. Try having more heart-to-hearts with your spouse. Developing your own spirituality, yoga practice, exercise routine, or arts-and-crafts projects can all be therapeutic. While this is an ending, it is also a beginning.

192. Prepare for Retirement

There are a number of things you can do to ensure a nice retirement for yourself. Find the level of planning that is right for you. First of all, create a steady income. Retirees with a traditional pension who get a monthly check for life have been found to be more content than those with the same level of wealth but only a 401(k). People feel more secure when they don't worry about outliving their money.

And retirees who have both a pension and a 401(k) are even happier, buoyed by the security of a guaranteed income plus a pool of cash to pay for unexpected expenses. Traditional pensions are going away, but you can create the equivalent of one on your own. You can invest a portion of your 401(k) or other savings in an "income annuity," which will pay you a guaranteed income for as long as you live.

Keep active—to a point. Staying engaged in a variety of activities also increases your shot at an enjoyable retirement. Retirees who both worked and volunteered are more likely to consider themselves very satisfied. But you can't hustle and bustle your way to retirement nirvana. The boost in satisfaction trailed off for retirees who worked or volunteered more than 200 hours a year, and the positive effect seemed to disappear at 500 hours. Motivation also mattered. People who worked because they needed the income, rather than for enjoyment, actually felt less satisfied about their retirement. The moral: Be careful that the activities you pursue don't become too much like, well, work.

When you retire, try to control your exit. People who leave their jobs voluntarily are 30 percent more likely to be happy in retirement than those who were pushed out. People who retire on their own schedules have had a better opportunity to get their post-work finances in order. They're also better prepared psychologically.

Of course, you can't control whether you'll have to stop working because of ill health or downsizing, which account for 75 percent of involuntary retirements. But while it's tough to think about, it pays to recognize the possibility and do some advance planning; say, looking into your options for taking Social Security and getting health insurance to tide you over until you qualify for Medicare. Then you won't be caught totally off guard.

Studies show older retirees tend to feel better about their lives than younger ones. So if you've tried to improve your situation and it still isn't going well, hang in there. Chances are that life, like fine wine, will improve with age.

193. Exercise

One of the best things that people can do to make themselves happier is to exercise regularly. Vigorous regular exercise helps you feel better about yourself and your life overall. This is something that regular exercisers know, but relatively few therapists and doctors prescribe. It works because the mind and the body are one interconnected entity. When you exercise regularly, you tone your body and metabolism, regulate stress hormones, and promote the release of endorphins.

There are many long-term benefits of exercise, like a lower blood pressure, improved strength and endurance, a trimmer physique and the confidence that follows, increased mental alertness, and a reduced risk of getting cancer, diabetes, and heart disease. But the bottom line here is that exercise simply makes you feel good.

Some say it has to be intense, or anaerobic (involving short energy bursts that cause the body to temporarily run out of oxygen), to bring on the psychological boost. But any workout you enjoy is part of the feel-good equation.

You need to keep variety in your exercise plan, too. The body always adapts, and you need to keep challenging it. So, vary the intensity, walk, bowl, play golf, cross-train, take dance classes, try a new sport, use a personal trainer for a few sessions, join a gym, lift weights, etc. Keep it fresh, and you will feel happier.

194. Things You Can Do for Yourself

Choose to be happy.
Be kind.
Appreciate the little things.
Be grateful.
Keep learning.
Exercise every day.
Spend less than you make.
Quit eating crap.
Care about other people; serve the wider world.

195. Happiness Reminders for Relationships

Make friends with yourself so you can be a good friend to others.
Be grateful for friends.
Be generous, loving, loyal, and tolerant.
Hug people whenever you can (and when it's appropriate).
Demonstrate your dedication and assurance of your commitment.
Develop deep listening.
Help others without thought of personal gain or getting thanked.
When it comes to friends, be a good forgetter.

196. Happiness Reminders for Work

Be mindful at work, whatever your tasks are.

Strive to do your work well.

Seek total absorption in tasks and use skillful effort.

Be as organized as possible.

Set goals.

Do your job with integrity and a healthy sense of humor.

Manage your time well.

Keep learning and improving your skills.

Accept your mistakes as human and learn from them.

Develop a mission.

Work to be disciplined and have self-control.

Practice ethical restraint and morality.

197. Happiness Reminders for Every Day

Smile when you awaken.

Wake with gratitude to the earth.

Make peace of mind and happiness your first priority.

Do each routine task mindfully.

Be thoughtful about what you feed your mind.

Stay in the present moment.

Practice patience and develop your ability to wait and listen.

Eat slowly and mindfully.

Speak kindly and with a sense of the best timing.

198. Happiness Reminders for Special Occasions

Live in the present moment, even if there is an occasion or event
you are looking forward to.

Prepare for an occasion with gratitude, kindness, and generosity.

Speak and act on only what is true and useful. Speak wisely and
appropriately.

Appreciate all the little things.

199. Happiness Reminders for Home Duties

Even in the garbage and dirty laundry, see beauty.

As you clean and do other duties, be mindful and in the present
moment.

Reduce clutter and seek simplicity.

Prepare food with love.

200. Happiness Reminders for Talking

Speech should be wise, kind, and minimal.

Talk only when necessary. Value silence.

Ask yourself if you need to express an opinion or make a
comment.

The quieter you become, the more you will hear.

Make telephone calls with awareness and mindfulness.

Apologize immediately if you were thoughtless or cruel.

Forgive yourself and others.

Offer advice only when asked, and then with compassion.

Do not lie.

Accept criticism, study it, then let it go.

Temper your anger. Arguing is useless.

Give accurate feedback.

Respond with humor.

201. Happiness Reminders for Health

Appreciate your body and what it allows you to do and experience.

Choose healthful food.

Exercise your body and mind every day.

Appreciate the aging process.

Remember that everything is impermanent, even sickness.

Stop, calm down, and rest to heal.

Do not abuse intoxicants.

202. Happiness Reminders for Nature

Appreciate all of nature, the sunrise and sunset and everything in between.

Breathe.

Embrace a natural way of living. Simplify.

Live in harmony with plants and animals.

Accept the change of weather, seasons, and environment.

Walk in peace on the earth.

Wish that all beings are happy, content, and at peace.

203. Happiness Reminders for Feelings

Choose happiness.

The present moment is all you have.

Be kind to all beings.

Ground yourself in moment-to-moment awareness.

See difficulties and suffering as teachers.

Resolve to practice moderation.

Overcome anger by developing compassion.

Accept circumstances with humor, calmness, or constructive effort.

Be generous.

Let go of fear and anxiety, through meditation.

React to unpleasantness with calm and equanimity.

Reduce or eliminate your expectations. Cling to nothing.

Practice conscious restraint with small desires to build your ability
   to deal with larger desires.

Resist less, grasp less, and identify with things less.

Choose a thoughtful response.

Develop patience.

Sow good seeds.

204. Happiness Reminders for Your Spiritual Path

Meditate.

Do breathing exercises.

Practice relaxation.

Do visualization exercises.

Be mindful, awake, aware, in the present moment.

Cultivate your faith.

Understand karma of action, speech, and thought.

Observe your thoughts but know that you are not them.

Be kind.

205. Books to Read, Web Sites to Access

14,000 Things to be Happy About

Self-Meditation

The Wish List

Instant Karma

Field Guide to Happiness

201 Little Buddhist Reminders

1,325 Buddhist Ways to be Happy

www.authentichappiness.org

www.myhappiness.com

www.selfgrowth.com

www.thingstobehappyabout.com

About the Author

Barbara Ann Kipfer has published more than forty books, including the best-selling *14,000 Things to be Happy About*, *Field Guide to Happiness* (Lyons Press), *Instant Karma*, and *8,789 Words of Wisdom*. She lives in Connecticut.